THE IMMORTAL NOW:

Ascension and the Nature of the Present Time

Patricia Grabow

Assisted by

Christine Kauffman and Charlotte McArthur

Book Publishers Network
P.O. Box 2256
Bothell • WA • 98041
PH • 425-483-3040
www.bookpublishersnetwork.com

10 9 8 7 6 5 4 3 2 1

Printed in the United States of America

ISBN10 1-887542-77-9
ISBN13 978-1-887542-77-7

Cover Designer: Laura Zugzda
Typographer: Stephanie Martindale

To our children and families and those we have found on our journeys. They have been truly soul mates, those to whom one does not have to explain one's search and whom one knew with the heart the moment of meeting. You have always been with us and we with you. Thank you for your faith in us.

To those to whom the books will have meaning, thank you for giving us this purpose.

Other books available by Patricia Grabow and At One Press

Messages from God: Passage from Fear—
Armageddon or Renaissance?

Messages from God: Passage from Karma—
A Coming Release from Sin and Repentance

www.patriciagrabow.com
www.theimmortalnow.com

email: patricia@theimmortalnow.com

Contents

FOREWORD

For all of the recorded history of mankind, Death has defined us, circumscribed our arts and philosophy, and given rise to our religions. In this third book, *Immortal Now*, Patricia Grabow has set forth the heady truths which can deliver us from that bondage. Here, she presents our choices. As individuals, we may choose a finite existence in a shadowy world, the world we think we live in, or we may embrace individual immortality in the timeless presence of love.

Immortal Now is an intriguing title which may be read as a demand, a prayer, a how-to-book, a description of a work that is part science and part mysticism, and all of the above. The book is, in every sense, a revolutionary work which redefines the interrelationships of the individual, the world, and the universe in a way that is both new and compelling. Out of those relationships spring concepts of timelessness and the eternal present, the nature of being, the nature of reality, and the power of love, all of which are central to individual immortality.

For many years now, certain neuropsychologists have taken it upon themselves to study the human brain in order to locate the source of religious euphoria and mysticism. More recently they seem to have found it in the geography of the right temporal lobe. They have proved to their own satisfaction that stimulation in this part of the brain enabled certain people to believe that they had made a connection with God. This location has been irreverently nicknamed "the God box" by waggish detractors.

In *Immortal Now*, "the God box" is located, not geographically but precisely, in the heart. The book teaches that the heart is the "point of omniscience" and of the capacity to love. The heart is "free of all fear, . . . a window to the universe." It is the heart which powers the ascension.

By the very nature of its subject, *Immortal Now* is not easily accessible to the reader. In order to describe the indescribable, to explain the inexplicable, to use language as a bridge to a kind of knowledge which language cannot delineate, the book has employed images that speak to common human experience. A child lost in contemplation of a flower, a would-be swimmer engulfed by a wave, an individual lost in the spectacle of a glorious sunset are summoned again and again to elucidate a state of timelessness, a surrender of self consciousness, the experience of love to the millionth power.

Immortal Now is not a book that we can just read, to pass the time, or for an evening's entertainment. It is a book that we wrestle with, and read again, and wrestle some more, until we experience a well-earned epiphany. It seems to raise more questions than it answers, but there will be answers.

What is the nature of this immortality? The book teaches that the individual is not born and does not die. Wow! Where does that leave us? Is this immortality like some kind of community cloud, or a tribe of wraiths wrapped in water vapor winding through treetops? No, it is not. First of all, immortality is an individual undertaking, and it is already happening. Individuals slip in and out of this consciousness all the time.

The book teaches that the world that we believe we live in, the world which is marked by evil doing and death, is no more real than the reflections in a mirror. How does that work? The Wizard of Oz and Plato's shadows on the wall of the cave come to mind, but they're no help at all. If this reality is the one that the individual appears to be born into and appears to die out of, what happens to the individual before he appears and after he disappears?

If that were not complicated enough, remember that immortality is not reserved for individuals only, but is available to all life, including that beautiful camellia bush, the carpenter bees at the back door, the chambered nautilus, and my dog Gus.

Those who do not know Patricia might reasonably ask how she came by this kind of knowledge. The answer is simple, and not simple. Patricia died in London, England on June 16, 1980 in a car accident. When she reluctantly returned to this life, she brought with her the gift of this and two other books coming through her. Patricia had been chosen for a particular journey, among kindly companions, also chosen, who would assist her in recording and publishing the truths which have culminated in *Immortal Now*.

Jay Booth
Author, teacher, friend

Introduction

We are all seekers of love and truth,(both of which may be the very same thing) yearning for the single solution to our craving for spiritual enlightenment and for peace and forgiveness in our soul. Beyond that, we are looking for the encouragement that mankind is on the brink of discovery. A new awareness that life on this planet does not have to be in turmoil and human suffering will end.

Precious few books, philosophies and organized religions have offered us little more than a glimpse of what might be.

In the following pages you will find the inspirational reality, the unadorned truth about life, love and the answers to what you have always believed, the truth you held in your heart about a God, a Supreme Being, a Universal spirit that lives in all of us. And it is so much more. It is the unveiling of the beauty and all-inclusive love that is our true essence. It is the foretelling of a new peaceful era, a gathering of kindred souls to create a new joyous spirit of life for all.

In short, you will see that you can be released from the imperfect words and ideas of the past and begin to see the eternal spirit as part of yourself without fear, restriction, without judgment, without punishment and without karmic debt. You will begin to see your real identity and your part in the creation of a new world.

Never has this information been more critical to each one of us than in this time of turmoil the globe over. The physical transition of the planet; the terrible pull towards tribalism as backlash in an age of enlightenment. Now more than ever we need to understand the compassionate and loving creative part we will all play in the shaping of the future; the exciting discovery process within the consciousness within the individual. It is the dream realized.

You will find out the most astonishing things about yourself and the power you possess. You will see yourself as you really exist and not the shadow self or the imagined self or the self you were taught to believe was you by family, schools and organized religion. They did not know, nor could they image the awesome being, so full of love and truth that you and they are.

Just for fun, try reading a few chapters aloud to yourself. You may find, as I did, that the material has a rhythm and a humor, not expected in such a serious work.

Rosie Porter,
Author, Newspaper publisher, and friend for 30 years.

Acknowledgements

First, to acknowledge and put into words the love to the millionth power I experienced when I died is not possible, but it must be done anyway. There are no words for the love and presence I have felt every day since that experience. It is like the essence of one's pure being which is always there in everyone and glows from a new compartment in the heart and is truly without a name, though throughout human history people have tried, in vain, to define it. Whatever it is, it is there and has become with joy my reason for existence. It is my hope that the reader will understand that there is no ego in that love. Allowing *The Immortal Now* to come through and publishing this book seems like part of a living prayer for me. My only motive and the single motive of those who have worked with me, has been gratitude.

The Immortal Now truly teaches that there is no death and that we are at a time when we are, as life – all life – beginning to understand that there is only the present. That is where we exist. The experience of mortality is like an image on a mirror of what we believe. There is a great deal of quantum physics in the book but it goes beyond that. The mirror projection where the life/death cycle appears, is not what life is. The veil that defines us as "mortal" is lifting; thus the subtitle of this book: The Ascension and the Nature of the Present Time. If there is no time, which the book tells us, then all life is lived in the present. Another point the book clarifies concerns preaching of the impending Armageddon by many Christian churches. This, in response to mega-million copies sold of a series of books on the end of the world and the people left behind after the "second coming." *The Immortal Now* is, in a sense, counter to those books and explains that the "second coming" is occurring, but not in the way described in some orthodox Christian interpretations. The veil is simply lifting, exposing the facts of existence in the present. It shows that we are collectively moving beyond the life/death cycle without fear, and no living thing is left behind.

A special thank you goes to Charlotte McArthur, her husband, Bruce McArthur, and their remarkable family who have participated in this work and stood by me and my family since the accident. It is fitting that this book come out at the celebration of Charlotte McArthur's life, April 26, 2008 with a gathering of great beings who have loved this amazing woman and the family she adored and nurtured. I truly owe my life to her and to them and will never really be able to repay that debt. In addition, acknowledgement and gratitude go to Christine Kauffman and her family who helped me with this book and upon whose daily prayers and faithful support I have come to depend. I have been surrounded by what the work calls "soul mates" and that is truly what they are. Rosie Porter and her family and Jay Booth, my dear, cynical, truly intellectual friends and who found so much in the work, and others including Barbara McCormick have been there as rocks

– truthful, kind and accepting. The daily presence of my family has been like the water to the fish, that in which I swam and upon which I depended entirely. It has been all of the life of my youngest son, Rob, and half of the lives of my two older sons in which this work has emerged. They have been understanding, questioning, funny, and most of all, patient, as this work has emerged. Thank you hardly seems adequate, I am so very grateful to have been given so much.

Patricia Grabow

SECTION ONE

1

PEACE

The ascension occurs within each individual, but it is not recognizable as such. It is not, "Lo here," or, "Lo there." It is within the individual being. It is not part of the social system or part of your experience with others. It is your experience with yourself, alone, that is why it is occurring within each individual. It is occurring in ways you cannot understand at this point, but there is not an individual left out. All are going through the ascension together.

The ascension occurs within each individual, but it is not recognizable as such.

If you were to have a mirror in front of you and the mirror reflected whatever you thought and the mirror showed whatever you perceived and the mirror showed whatever you believed, that mirror is not you. That mirror is only reflecting whatever thought you have at that moment. It is like a pin-point in time reflecting that moment. Is the mirror you? No, it is not.

That is the world at this point reflecting the belief systems and the understandings and the experiences of the individuals and, collectively, experiences within each individual and their relationship to God. It is not the world. It is in the world. Their relationship to God is going on continuously within them, not within the mirror. The world experience that you call "reality" is the mirror. The experience that is going on is within your larger being and recounts your human experience. It is not your nature. Your nature is outside the mirror. Your nature is the love that you feel—the joy that exists within. Do you affect the mirror is the question.

There is great, great turmoil at this point. The Middle East is the area of the world in which the great messages have come. It is impossible for you to fathom the nature of the turbulence that is being experienced. What you do physically, affects that area. Do you affect the mirror, which is the Middle East, which is the mirror? That is the question and the answer is, "Yes, you do." What exists for you, as a being, is your nature. The mirror is the outward manifestation. You understand this more, and more, and more. And when you move to the place of your own being, you move further and further away from the mirror, so that the mirror is very distant at times and the experience that is being affected is very distant at times. You remain who you are. You remain what you are. You are unaffected by the mirror. The only thing you affect is the mirror itself. The reality is you and the present. There is no other reality. You appear here when you are born. You leave here when you die. Is that the only reality? What exists is like a ray of sunshine that creates the light that creates the reflection that creates the image within the world. Do you affect the image within the world? Yes, you do. Is it the truth? No it is not. You will deal with that which exists and it is important at this time. It is important that you understand what exists and what does not. It is terribly important that the world understands and makes that distinction because they are ascending... because the world is in a stage of ascension. Does it need the reflection? No, it does not. The mirror remains. You remain, but the image is altered completely. Present time remains the present time. The image that is created within the mirror is completely altered. Jesus understood this and attempted to show that the world could be left and returned to and that it would not affect the nature of the individual. The choice was made to ignore that part of the affected. The choice was made to stay within what was termed "reality." Was it reality? No. But, the choice was made to stay in the picture that was being presented. Was it the nature of the individual? No, but it was a choice. Choices are being made now in the reflected being to leave the perceptions that created the image. Love that is felt in meditation is overwhelming and you could not remain here should you try to stay here with that love, so you leave. So you let the mirror become light as you leave so that you can experience that love, more, and more, and more. It is important that you allow that love to occur now. It is not necessary to stay in the world at this point.

Symbols: You could call this plane of existence a symbolic plane. Words, images, feelings about images, objects—but God within a theological base is still symbology. It is the time in which you separate symbology from reality

There is much joy in finding the nature of who you are. You deal in symbols here on this plane of existence. Symbology is everything. You could call this plane of existence a symbolic plane. Words, images, feelings about images, objects—but God within a theological base is still symbology. It is the time in which you separate symbology from reality.

Is a time of leaving symbols behind—countries, plants, flags, trees—all symbols of reality. To know the reality of the tree is to see beyond symbol. There is spirit within the tree. There is life within the tree. There is soul within the tree. As you move to higher planes of consciousness within the present time, you see the other elements of the tree. It is by glimpse. The only place in which you do not deal in symbology is within love. The heart does not deal in symbology. And in meditation, you are removed from symbols. At that point you are at peace and at one within the present. It is difficult to understand why symbols have become so important. Imagine that you are a blind person. You have symbols within your own consciousness, which allow you to understand reality. They are of the past. It is difficult to understand how you see a tree. When you are at one with the tree and love the tree, you are in the present with the tree. When you remember the tree, and the symbol of the tree, you are no longer in the present with the tree. What the ascension is, truly, is moving into the present. It is difficult to imagine—in the present—all of time, but it is joy, and peace, and everything that theologians have discussed as they promote the symbol of the present.

In order for the Middle East to achieve peace, it has to clarify the picture of what peace actually is within the individual being.

It is like being present with the tree. It is a joyous process.

The peace you seek is not on the mirror and is outside of what you believe. It is like a child who has not yet learned to run and trying to understand what it is like to run a marathon. The child only understands what they are able to. The projection that exists out there is like the projection of the child. It is simple. It is not accurate. In order for the Middle East to achieve peace, it has to clarify the picture of what peace actually is within the individual being. The books help to see what that picture consists of and it does not consist of what the child has thus far projected out there. The problem, to some degree, is the way that the individuals are taught do this. They are reaching the point where they are no longer projecting out on the mirror, but exist within themselves. It is like there is a timeline between what is actually happening during the ascension process and what is perceived to be happening out there upon the earth. It is not the same. You will reach a point where you will let the mirror become obsolete. It is what is happening during meditation. It is the movement to a location that is called the ascension—to the point where there is only present time. The projection, the language, the image is your own being which is inclusive of all. It is happening rapidly. They have worn out. They have lost their meaning. They have lost their understanding. They have lost their being. They have lost their life. It is like a plant that is no longer growing. It is blown away. It is like the analogy of scales before the eyes because the scales no longer exist. They are tapped. They no longer carry any meaning. You perceive this within your being, but you do not understand it yet.

The ascension has brought up so many themes. It will be in so many years and the world will end. The world does not end. The perception of the individual is all there is. It is a moment. It is in the twinkling of an eye. It is all of the time. It is the moment in which there is nothing but God.

It is sought in everything the individual does. You will see it is the image that Jesus attempted to teach through words. It is not attainable through words, because of the nature of time.

Time is the projection on the mirror and, therefore, to teach the understanding of what the second coming is, is not to understand in words. Words will bring a connection and it is the connection as the reading occurs. It is like being lost in a moment and in that moment there is no time and yet it is possible to use words to bring one to that actual experience and, therefore, that is the reason for these messages coming through a book. The experience of reading a book is the nature of what is being achieved and not the words themselves and that is why the books are not to be quoted in any way because the words will only transfer the being back into an image within the mirror and pull them away from the experience of what is actually happening as one transcends this experience. It is ironic that that is the nature of how it works, but it is. When you transcend your experience here, you do not leave your experience here. It is a difficult concept to understand, but it actually occurs that way. The experience here remains an experience, but the transcendence actually occurs momentarily. It is a freedom that occurs for the individual and collectively. It is a freedom that occurs for humankind and all life. The transcendence is occurring in the present time. It is occurring within the now. It is always occurring within the present time. It is always occurring. That is why Jesus could say, "Before Abraham was, I am," because that is the nature of the being, but it is the belief systems that have been projected on to the mirror that limit the ascension. It is losing all credibility among all of those who understand. It is a difficult concept to understand but it is the nature of reality.

It will be in so many years and the world will end. The world does not end. The perception of the individual is all there is.

It affects everything. It affects animals. It affects children. It affects the stars. It affects the sky. There is nothing that is not affected by it.

The way will become clear as you progress rapidly. Prayer is effective. You assume that prayers that have been given in the Middle East, but they have been in ways you do not understand. The prayer that has been given is like an arrow piercing through the belief system of the world. It is reaching in to the dimension of which we speak when we discuss the ascension. It is breaking the barrier of the human belief system. It is important that all prayers be acknowledged and understood as a means by which to ascend. They are a vehicle for the ascension and cannot be discounted by those who seek only intellectual answers to problems. You will learn to pray effectively in many, many ways and the guidance will come from within. In many, many religions, there is prayer that involves meditation, that is connection with the higher being in ways that you still do not quite understand. That meditation is the means by which the veil is pierced at this point.

The ascension involved the dropping away of scales before the eyes of the individual. It has been characterized as the veil. It has been characterized as many, many, many things, but it is simply the dropping away of an entire belief system. That belief system is no longer. Thus, many are understanding that the churches, the institution, the human belief in which so many have invested with their hearts and their minds are dropping away. They are not to be grieved for. It is a natural process and it is the ascension so they are to leave gracefully in your experience.

The love that you feel within your heart is the only reality; as that love expands relinquish your beliefs about the nature of God, and the nature of your experience, and nature of reality, and the nature of life itself. It is a freedom that cannot even be touched by words, but occurs momentarily frequently and for the individual. It is the coming of the new age, the coming of the new period, the coming of enlightenment universally. It is the dream of so many for so very long. It is the result of eons and eons of prayer beyond what you even understand. It is the longing of the heart on a daily basis. It is effective because it permeates all life. All life seeks the same enlightenment. Symbolically, plants seek the light. Human beings seek light through the life of the plants. It is symbolic. It is not what you term reality. The deeper, deeper reality is the love that you feel when you look upon a child or watch a sunset or look into the eyes of someone that you dearly love. That is reality. That is the underlying reality and the only place that the individual exists is within that reality on a global basis. Imagine that the world reaches a point where all it feels is love. Imagine that the anger, the revenge, the distrust—all of those things simply vanish. It is not a loss as so many of the traditional religions have characterized it. It is a freedom beyond your wildest imagination. You will miss nothing. You will not even notice its loss. The world is ready for this remarkable transformation. It seeks it in the present time. It does not seek it in the future. At every moment of all life, there is the seeking of that joy, of that light, of that love.

To understand the present time is truly to understand the nature of love for both are totally one. You will also see the dropping away of any sense of the past. In the present time, there is no past, there is no future, there is only the present, and yet it contains everything within the past and everything within the future. Imagine a world in which there is no past and there is no future. Imagine a world in which there is no good, there is no evil. Imagine a world in which the love of children is the only love that you feel—the joy, the peace, the unconditional surrender to love itself. That is the experience that the world is entering. The mirror is giving way to the prayers of the world and the ascension is occurring.

The road to peace is a personal road. It is not within a group consciousness. it is within an individual consciousness. When the world longs for peace, it truly longs for it within each individual. It is a spiritual goal, not a group goal, so world peace is not possible. What is possible is individual peace and the world reflects that individual peace. It is a spiritual goal, not a group goal, so world peace is not possible. What is possible is individual peace and the world reflects that individual peace. It is important to make that distinction at this time because the goal is peace within the individual. Whatever contributes to that peace contributes to the world situation. For example, if an individual finds himself in a position of being in conflict in a war-like situation, that is a reflection of the turmoil within the group consciousness. It is a collective identity. It is a collective theology. It is a collective perception of the world. However, if each individual within that situation were to only turn to prayer ten minutes every hour, the conflict would be resolved with the power of prayer of to pierce the veil, to reflect on the mirror that which the individual truly believes. It is important to make this important distinction because the type of prayer is of no importance—if it Muslim, if it is Christian, or any denomination. It is only the heart that exits anyway and so if the heart seeks that connection with the divine within, then that is manifest, for example, in the image of the mirror.

It is important for the entire world at this time to truly understand that it is not important as to what the denomination is. It is only the function of the being that exists within the heart. In the ascension, that is what is occurring within the present time. It is nothing that is contrived out there. It is always occurring always within the heart. The heart is always seeking peace. The heart is always seeking love. The heart is always seeking its own nature. It is not something that exists outside. It is something that exists within and is ultimately projected out into the world so that the world can see it. The question has to be asked, "Why then would we not just simply exist within the heart and not attempt to create a world out there that reflects any of the elements of the heart?"

The world is the reflection of a belief system. The operative word is system. It is a perception. It is a paradigm. It is a system. It is a symbolic understanding of what is perceived only. As the individual moves away from their own understanding of the present time—which they have understood since birth when they loved—they move into a symbolic system depending on where they were born, under which theological base they were born, in what part of the world they were born, and it is only their appearing within a system, within a context, within a paradigm. Their appearing has little to do with their nature. They are appearing like an image on a mirror. They are appearing. The system then controls the nature of appearance—the colors, the hues, the manifestations of their appearing, but it is not within their nature.

To begin to understand the nature of the individual, is to begin to understand what God is—what Love is, what Truth is, what Principle is, what Mind is, what everything is because that is all that truly is. Love is all there is. There is nothing else.

The world is ready to truly see the individual, not the symbol of the individual. The "second coming" is occurring within the love that exists is undeniable. It is like a ray of light that shines upon the mirror and the only thing, ultimately, that is seen by the mirror is that light. The mirror is transformed, but the light has always been there. The image on the mirror is that unconditional love. When the Bible discusses the world dropping away, that is essentially what happens. The image on the mirror drops away and the mirror is filled with light. It is like when Patricia left the earth and came back. The light was all there was. It is nothing to be feared. The image on the mirror was not the truth. The image on the mirror was only a symbol of the individual. It was not the nature of the individual. All life is symbolic. All life is kingdoms. All life is paradigms, but the underlying truth is the unconditional light of Love. Those who have gone before and returned have understood this about the nature of life. They have attempted to bring it back to the paradigm and discuss it in symbols so that the individuals who are existing within those symbols can understand the nature of Love. It is seen in glimpses at this point, but, like water breaking through a dam, the dam is giving way. The paradigms are giving way. The light is permeating everything.

When individuals have talked about polar shifts they do not understand that that has already occurred within consciousness. The center for spiritual revelation was the Middle East. It is no longer. And the battles have to do with their belief that it is still the center. Unlimited Love is permeating all of it.

Each individual is becoming enormously psychic, is becoming enormously connected, is becoming aware of what is happening and rejoices that it is happening at last. There is a reason that these books are coming through where they are coming through. It is like the earth has shifted. When individuals have talked about polar shifts they do not understand that that has already occurred within consciousness. The center for spiritual revelation was the Middle East. It is no longer. And the battles have to do with their belief that it is still the center. Unlimited Love is permeating all of it. What is not understood is that it involves all life—that it involves grain and plants and elephants and trees and all life. It is like the child who is learning to walk, not understanding the marathon, it is impossible still to perceive, but as the light permeates everything at once, then it is of no consequence that the child did not understand what they were beginning on a path to experience.

You will see that the way is like a stream opening into an ocean. The stream is part of the ocean, but it becomes so much more massive. It is like the collective awareness as it begins to expand. The awareness becomes so overwhelming that it cannot be stopped. The need of the individual to revert to the old ways, the old identities, the old paradigms, the old religions, the old faith gives way to the ascension. It is ironic that churches have preached the ascension, but they are not part of the ascension. The ascension is like the ocean. It is covering everything. It is a child who is suddenly lost in watching a flower. It is not that the child ceases to exist. The child exists, but the child is lost in watching the flower. The child is not thinking of himself as a given entity. He is thinking only of the moment that he is lost in the flower. The old ways give way. It is not because the individual is no longer devout or loving or prayerful. It is that the individual is no longer aware of a given religious identity or a given family identity or a given national identity. It is that the individual is aware of the love that is there. It is a momentary thing and like all momentary things, it contains within itself all that there is.

You will see that the way is like a stream opening into an ocean. The stream is part of the ocean, but it becomes so much more massive.

Within the belief system of time, one assumes that life occurs within time—that is you are a child at three years old and then you come back to yourself and progress to being an older individual. That is not the way it works. What is in reality—what exists is that the child is the child and the moment at which the child is lost in the flower is the moment at which the child is at one with themselves and the universe.

It is a different view and it is almost as though that moment becomes all there is and exists within the present time. When we recall loving someone completely, that moment is forever. It is not that that is ever dissolved. It is never dissolved. It does not dissolve, as the individual never dissolves. The child lives much more within the present. When the child has more and more experiences within this plane of existence. Existence isn't that the individual becomes older. The individual becomes more and more attached to this plane of existence. There is no time. It is a difficult concept for you to understand, but there is no time. Time does not exist. It is like watching a movie and saying that within this movie, there will be time and then the time exists within that movie. So within this plane of existence, one assumes there is time and as the individual becomes older, they get older. It is not so. It is important not to discount reality. That is not how it actually happens. It is just that those moments become more and more frequent—the moments like the child who is lost in the flower become more and more and more frequent until there is only present time and it is filled with that consciousness. That is how the shift occurs. It is difficult to envision this shift because within this paradigm, the churches have removed themselves from the truth of their own power, their own existence, their own strength, their own glory. This is not to judge them in any way. It is only the truth of the paradigm.

You will see that there is much to be seen within the sunset—that there is light. There is life. There is rain. There is shadow. There is remarkable complexity to it. It is not simple. Love is not simple. Love is complex. Love is varied. Love is unique to each individual. It is not as you envision it at this point. You will use the light and see the complexity of the paradigms that is coming, the world that are coming—the ascension.

You will see that there is much to be seen within the sunset—that there is light. There is life. There is rain. There is shadow. There is remarkable complexity to it. It is not simple. Love is not simple. Love is complex. Love is varied. Love is unique to each individual. It is not as you envision it at this point. You will use the light and see the complexity of the paradigms that is coming, the world that are coming—the ascension.

You will see that it is not part of this experience to understand all of this experience. It is like the individual has chosen to see reality in pieces rather than as the whole picture. Because of that it is confusing. To those who seek what has been termed "world peace." The pieces are more than can be numbered. It is like the puzzle that has a thousand pieces. For each piece to try to understand the entire picture, it does not make sense necessarily. What happens when one meditates is that the entire picture is visible and understandable. It is like the entire picture is accessible to the individual at that point. And when the individual returns from meditation, the peace that the individual experiences is that which comes from understanding the entire picture.

It is a fragmented existence to the individuals. They are functioning on literally thousands of planes of existence at any point. It is difficult for you to understand how totally remarkable each individual is in the eyes of the Divine heart of themselves. There is that understanding and it exists on a different level. When one meditates, one is also able to see that as well.

The world is ready to see the entire picture. The frustration, the anger, the separateness, the lack of continuity for so many has become intolerable at this point. They seek that which exists within more than at any point in any history, anywhere. And they see the other side. It is like standing on the top of a mountain and watching a beautiful sunset. It is accessible. It is visible. It can be seen. It can be understood. And, it is beginning to be appreciated more, and more. The pain humanity is experiencing at this point is like the pain of the addict. They finally reach a point where they no longer wish to experience the kind of pain that they have been experiencing and, therefore, they turn within to themselves and find that all exists and all is peace and all is what has been understood to be the love they have sought all their life. It exists within the heart. It is important the world understands that is all there ever was. There never was anything but the heart. There was never anything but unlimited love. It is accessible like the sunset. It is accessible in Gaza. It is accessible in Pakistan. It is accessible in Iraq. It is accessible on the streets. It is accessible within the life of every living being. It is accessible to animals. It is accessible to plants. It is accessible to every form of life. It exists. World is reaching *the* point where it makes a shift. There are those who seek a date, a time, a moment. They do not understand the nature of the present time. Within the present time, that moment exists, has always existed, and always will exist. There is nothing but that moment within the present time. This is the hardest part for individuals to understand because they are so imbued with the theology that has created their world view. You will use the light and find that moment within your own experience. Within your own experience, that moment *is* all there is. There is nothing else.

You will see that there is much to be seen within the sunset: That is there is light. There is life. There is rain. There is shadow. There is remarkable complexity to it. It is not simple. Love is not simple. Love is complex. Love is varied. Love is unique to each individual. It is not as you envision it at this point. You will use the light and see the complexity of the paradigms that are coming, the world that is coming—the ascension. You will use the light and within your own being, you will see where revelation occurs. It occurs within. It does not occur without.

You will use the light and within your own being, you will see where revelation occurs. It occurs within. It does not occur without.

You will see that the pain and the suffering and the concern, the lack of problem solving, and all of the frustrations that are being experienced are there because it is like the residue that is being swept away. It has to come to the surface first and then it is able to be swept away by the spiritual. You will see that the Middle East is the cradle of civilization within this plane, but it is not the cradle of civilization as it exists. It is only a place. It is only a location within a paradigm. It is not the center for love. It is not the center for truth or any other revelation. It is only a place. It is only a moment within a moment within a moment that inspiration occurred for humanity, but the place that exists within the heart has always existed, will always exist and it is the center for spiritual revelation. It is not within a given location, upon this plane of existence, within this paradigm. It is too, too simple to even imagine. You will see that it is to be given respect, but it is only that. It is not where answers come. You will use the light and within your own being, you will see where revelation occurs. It occurs within. It does not occur without. It only exists within. It does not exist without. This is a concept that is very difficult for you on this plane of existence because you have always assumed that what is without is what exists and what is within is amorphous. At best, this is not the case. What is without is amorphous and what exists within is solid, is true. Within is reality. Within is peace. Within is where problems are solved and all solutions are reached. Within is where love is felt. Within is where all that exists happens.

The world is ready for its own understanding of the nature of the ascension and, most importantly, the nature of reality. It is like a story that was told about how the world exists, a myth, and the world that the individual is experiencing is different from the myth. It is like the world is the myth and reality is the heart. Reality is all there is. The myth is superficial to the breadth, and the depth, and the living that is occurring. Life is not within the myth. Life is within each individual, living being. The world, as you experience it within the present time, is all there is. There is no time. There is no system. There is no theology. There is only life. The heart is the vehicle by which understanding occurs. It is the vehicle by which life occurs. The heart is the substance of each individual. To assume that the image on the mirror or the myth is reality, is to believe that they are all that is real, so that when one dies from the image on the mirror, one assumes that the individual is no longer there and that is not the case. The individual is there. The individual neither appeared on the mirror, nor did they

It is like a story that was told about how the world exists, a myth, and the world that the individual is experiencing is different from the myth.

leave the mirror. They simply exist. The image is the projection of this being on the mirror. The grief that occurs when the image leaves the mirror is part of the image projected on the mirror. The individual exists. There is nothing but that existence. When one transcends the mirror, one transcends only the image. They do not transcend themselves, because they exist. Great masters have taught this. They have understood the nature of being. They have understood the nature of reality. They have understood that the ascension is only the transcendence of the image, not reality, therefore, exists from generation, to generation, to generation, to generation. It is important at this time that you understand this to be true. The generation, to generation, to generation part of the myth is no longer germane to the life that exists. The life that exists is all there is. As humanity transcends the image, humanity simply returns to its own nature. The ascension is not as theology has taught; that is, that there are great beings and then they ascend. All life is that being. All life is that ascension. All life is that image. All life is in existence. What happens with the ascension is that state of being that is inherent within each individual simply stays.

There are moments in each life. They come and they go. The only difference is what theology has termed the ascension - that that state of existence that is pure love, that is pure light, that is pure self, that is pure being - stays and does not leave. The image no longer appears on the mirror and then disappears. It simply exists. It is ecstasy beyond anything that you can fathom and like the child that is learning to walk and cannot envision the marathon, you cannot yet quite envision what this truly means in your experience, but you sense it and each being on this plane of existence senses it. It is an intuitive understanding; it is not an intellectual understanding. Therefore, when one reads, for example, these books, one experiences that enlightenment, that transcendency, that understanding, but one does not intellectually say, "Aha, I have reached that point. I have now ascended."

That is not the nature of being. It is only the nature of the theology that is being taught. Symbols are of great importance on this plane of existence. As we discussed earlier, they are more than that. They are symbolic of the "you" of each individual, of each plant, of each animal, of each molecule. They are symbolic of reality. They are not reality because reality exists within the light of love. That is the nature of reality: Is only within the light of love. The light of love exists everywhere, all the time, in all places. There is no darkness. There is nothing that is not the light of love.

All life is in a state of transformation, of prayer, of awe at this time.

You will see that the light of love is within your experience in multiple ways, at multiple levels, all the time now. It is like a blossom that emerges on a flower. The flower's energy goes into the creation of the blossom. The energy of your life, at this point, is all going into the creation of the vehicle for understanding what all life is going through now. It is important that your lives focus on the blossom. The blossom emerges in its beauty and grandeur that was unseen before. They are visible at this point. It is more than a projection on a mirror because the beauty of a flower actually transcends the actual image of the flower. You are in a point of blossoming and emerging with "the peace that passes all understanding." It is within.

The world is in turmoil. The world is puzzled. The world does not understand itself at all now. The world does not see itself at all now. The world goes through the motions of attempting intellectually to understand itself, but the spiritual substance of its understanding, the peace, the joy, the blossom, is not there. It is within. It is as though, at this point, the world has tried to put its own being out there on the mirror so it assumes that the only thing left is the image on the mirror. That is not so. It is that an image on the mirror is losing its sparkle, its attraction, its power, its strength and what happens is that within each being, the joy, the blossom, the beauty, the strength, the power, the might is all emerging. It is important that these books come out at this point so there is that understanding of what is actually happening in reality. The present time is all there is ultimately and the movement into the present time is what is happening. The blossom is beyond beauty that you could imagine. It is beyond your understanding at this point, but, intuitively, you sense it. You feel it and in a meditative state, you experience it. When you come out of a meditative state, you see it only in glimpses at this point, but there is understanding.

The world is at war. The world is in turmoil. The world is puzzled. The world is seeing itself and understanding that its projection on the mirror is not the same as what exists within each being, so it is beginning to turn away from that projection into its own development, its own ascension. As that focus changes from creating a perfect society, or a perfect world, or a perfect relationship, or a perfect anything outside of the being within, the individual then begins to develop that which is going on within their own being. That does not mean that there is not love in the world. It does not mean that there is not truth, or kindness, or joy, or peace. It means that within each individual, as they place all of their energy in this blossoming within, that love, that kindness, that peace emerges truthfully to the world. The individual no longer seeks the truth outside its own being. It knows that the truth exists within. It is sufficient that that is a possibility at this point since that is not well understood—not that the flower understands what it is going to become as it begins to emerge.

The world is making a giant transformation. It is impossible for you to fathom the nature of this transformation, but it has never been experienced before, nor will it ever be experienced again. It is within the moment and it is implosive and explosive at the same time. The flower is emerging. It cannot be stopped. It shall not be stopped. It is not within the nature of the flower to be stopped. It is part of the growth of that flower that emerges from within. All life is in a state of transformation, of prayer, of awe at this time. There is no satisfaction outside of the self within. It is like the moment that the child observes the flower. The child is lost in the flower and more and more each individual is lost in the beauty of the flower and emerges into the nature of the present time. There ceases to be self. There ceases to be war. There ceases to be turmoil and strife. There only exists the child and the moment.

The world is making its giant transformation. It is impossible for you to fathom the nature of this transformation, but it has never been experienced before, nor will it ever be experienced again. It is within the moment and it is implosive and explosive at the same time. The flower is emerging.

You will see that the time that you envision for what is called the "second coming" and the ascension is different from the way it actually works. You assume that you are in a time framework, not only personally, but collectively as well, and the time framework allows for generational progression and over generation, after generation, after generation there is somehow ascension. It is almost as though you assume that the world is made up of moments of time called a generation. This is a concept that is so ingrained within your consciousness that it will take a movement within consciousness greater than you have ever assumed could happen, but it can happen within an instant. The instant is all there is. It is not as though generations built up, built up, built up. There were masters and the generations built up, built up again and then the final master would come. It is disappointing that this is not the nature of reality, but the masters of whom you speak so frequently understood that that was not the nature of reality.

You are the Divine, the child of the living God. That is not theory. That is the nature of reality.

There is nothing but the truth. There is nothing but love. There is nothing but the Divine Consciousness and the assumptions that you are a limited mortal limited to generational progression is based upon the theology that you are a limited mortal.

You are the Divine, the child of the living God. That is not a theory. That is the nature of reality. You are the child of the living. There is nothing but the living. There is no death. There is only life and its manifestation. There is nothing but the Divine. That is not something that occurs for some and not for others. There is nothing but the Divine. The nature of reality is Divine. The way to understand the Divinity within is simply to take the moment that the child sees the flowers and understand that experience. The child is lost in the flower. And, as living beings, you are lost in the Divine.

This concept is difficult because the world needs, at this point, to perpetuate the concept of limited mortal until it tires of it. When it tires of it, that moment occurs in which the child is lost in flower and there is nothing but the nature of the child and the nature of the universe. You are in a transitional period within your own consciousness, not within the image projected on the mirror, but within your own being. Your own being is exploding and imploding at the same time. It is difficult to handle this for many and they seek to find solace within the old theological terminology and view of the world, but they have chosen collectively not to return to those concepts. They have chosen to ascend. It is within their nature to do so. That ascension will affect everything that you see, you hear, and you experience. That ascension will impact the image on the mirror as well as the image within. It is as if you have reached a point where you can actually connect with your own being on a regular basis. It is nothing that you necessarily choose to do—you simply do it without even thinking. It is the moment that you look at the world and sigh a sigh of relief that that is not all there is. You understand that at this point and, collectively, have reached a point where you are at the cusp of that enormous transition.

The world is ready for these books and the awareness that exists within each individual. It has never been at the point of readiness as it is now. It sees both worlds. It understands both worlds. It can translate both worlds within its own experience. That has never occurred within the generational experience before except through the eyes of the masters. It is the "second coming" within each individual, so the eyes of the masters are viewing the world through the eyes of each individual. There are no specific individuals that are doing this. This is a universal experience. It is as though the great masters are within each individual, because the translation of the nature of their own being is being seen without being seen "through a glass, darkly." The glass is not stopping the understanding that exists within the individual. You will see that translates into the unheard of possibility that there could be peace within each individual and that places like the Middle East could actually transcend their own experience. It is uplifting to individuals to even think of that as a possibility, but it is a reality. "All things are possible unto God," means that all things are simply possible within the moment. That happens, not consciously, but unconsciously like the child that is lost in the flower. The child is not saying, "I will now be lost in the flower." It simply occurs and it occurs naturally and it occurs within each moment that that experience occurs for the child. It is important to understand that there is nothing else. It is important for you to understand that this is the time of what theologians call "salvation." It is not as if you lived a good life in a generational experience, it is that within the moment, you are free and have transcended the experience.

You will see that there is so very much that you understand and that cannot articulate because there are simply no words with which to articulate the experience. The experience is new to life. It is new in the sense that it is intensified. If you had an experience and then multiplied that by a quantum amount, you would have difficulty explaining the experience, but the experience is nonetheless there. It is part of the flow of life, itself so that is within your experience at this time. "There is nothing new under the son." That is true. There is nothing new in your experience that is not occurring within. But,

The linear delineations are part of the theological base. They are part of the creation of the kingdoms within the genesis of human concepts. However, it is still the image projected on the mirror and not the nature of reality. It is important for you to understand that the nature of reality is all there is.

the articulation of that within the realm of words that is collectively understood is simply more difficult. That is why the vision becomes one of image as opposed to specific articulated ideas. The image of the child is an image. It is a universal image to those who have experienced it and, therefore, they can understand it and the nature of the child. It much the same way, it is difficult to articulate what happens within all life, because all life is experiencing the same experience. One assumes that you have had an enlightened moment and that others have not. That is not so. Within each individual that is occurring always. It is the individual at one and at peace with their own being. It is not an experience that can necessarily be articulated and the kingdoms of life, for example, animals or plants or bug, or any other kingdom of life cannot articulate in same way, but the experience is universal. It is the nature of life itself within the present time. The linear delineations are part of the theological base. They are part of the creation of the kingdoms within the genesis of human concepts. However, it is still the image projected on the mirror and not the nature of reality. It is important for you to understand that the nature of reality is all there is. The image is important to individuals, but the need for the image is simply fading. The need for the words that simply articulate what you already know is fading and the words are simply becoming inadequate at this time and, therefore, what happens is that the individual understands this, accepts this, and allows the experience to flow. It allows the energy to flow. It allows life to flow. It allows the truth to flow. It allows the love within to simply flow.

That moment at which the love, and the light, and the truth is all flowing and the energy is flowing within the individual, is the moment of Divinity. It is the nature of Divinity. It is the truth of Divinity. It is an indomitable truth. It is truth that is not necessarily articulated nor will it ever again have a religious movement, per se. It is within. It is not outside the individual in a creed. It is not outside the individual in a person. It is not outside the individual in any form except in the form of the light of love. It is within the individual.

It is a welcomed time for humanity. The burden that has been carried for so long by humanity itself: the sadness, the grief, the guilt, that pain, the fear—all of those unnecessary burdens are being released from the experience of the individual. You will see that you will have freedom beyond your wildest imagination. The joy that occurs when that freedom happens is inarticulate joy. It is the presence of the divine within. It is like a child that comes home.

It is the peace of coming home. It is the comfort of coming home. It is the security of coming home. It is the joy of coming home. It is the quiet of coming home. It is not to be feared in any form. It is only to be experienced.

You will see that when the individual sees the vision of their own nature and the nature of what has been called God, it is explosive. It is like nothing they have ever known and it permeates their entire being. There is nothing within their being that is not effected. The child that has emerged from the fog, sees the vision and, at that point, will never return to the fog, to the limited sense of who they are or what their experience is because the child is not blinded an more. The term "scales have fallen from their eyes" is appropriate in this situation, because the scales that are referred to in the Bible are simply the image that is on the mirror and the image is covered over with belief after belief after belief. The crystalline form of the individual is what exists. The beliefs are only the scales, the limits, the beliefs surrounding the individual. As the individual then sees clearly, the need for pain, or sorrow, or unkindness, or all of the things that, by choice, within a belief system—and the need for those things has disappeared, never to return—*never to return.*

There are then no beliefs of multiple lives, generational systems, reincarnation, the scales, the limits are simply gone. The fog is gone. The limits have disappeared.

The most difficult concept to understand is that the transformation occurs within a millisecond. It is not something that occurs over many laborious lives, and mistakes, and difficulties. It is like the sun that has burst out of the clouds. It has all of the energy of the sun. It has all of the life-giving elements of the sun. The clouds did not limit that capacity of the sun. It simply covered it over temporarily. You will see that prophets have always seen this and understood. Then they told those who are lost within their own belief systems that the sun existed; that the light of love was the nature of the individual, that there was no death, that there was no generational system. There was only that which always existed, that which always nurtured, that which always gave life, that which was always forever within.

The term "scales have fallen from their eyes" is appropriate in this situation, because the scales that are referred to in the Bible are simply the image that is on the mirror and the image is covered over with belief after belief after belief. The crystalline form of the individual is what exists. The beliefs are only the scales, the limits, the beliefs surrounding the individual.

The reason the generational system remained was the nature of the love that exists between those who generate the children and the love between the parents and the children. But that love simply exists like the energy of the sun. It exists within the moment. As a parent looks upon a beautiful sleeping child, that moment exists. Those moments simply do not go away, return, go away, return. That moment exists within the individual. It does not exist outside the individual. It simply exists within the individual and continues to do so.

The world is aware of this. The world is aware of its antithesis as well. These are choices that individuals are making, but simply not on a conscious level. It is on a spiritual level that all choices are made.

Life is prayer. Life is joy. Life is the nature of the individual. The struggle within the Middle East is the belief that life is outside the individual. It has become more and more predominant and that the belief systems are of the most importance, not the life of the individuals. It is a critical issue at this point. Life is not destructible so that the individual is not destroyed, the nature is not destroyed, love of the individual for their families is not destroyed even though it seems impossible at a critical stage.

You will see that the way is becoming clearer every day. You will see that the path you are to follow becomes more and more prepared. It is becoming easier to follow the path you must follow in order to allow others to see the vision of the ascension. You will see that as the individual struggles, they only struggle within their own consciousness. It seems as though they are struggling within the "real world," but the struggle that takes place is within the inner being and the struggle within the world is also within its own inner being. It does not see the nature of the struggle, because it sees visually, but the visual image is only the outward symptom of the exceptionally complex process within each individual as they assess their understanding of God, as they express their love, as they feel love, as they seek to overcome limits within the "real world," but the struggle does not exist within the mirror. It only exists within each individual. When one encounters tremendous pain, as is going on now within certain countries of the Middle East, one see the pain is the pain of Armageddon in the individual—not outside of the individual. Biblical prophesy only discusses the outward visual effect, but that is not where it occurs. It occurs within the level of personal crisis. There is nothing exterior to the individual, so those crises occur within, not without. When that perspective is understood, then the experience is understood. You will see that as consciousness has shifted to the area in which the books are occurring, you will see the peace, the joy, the understanding that is occurring is again occurring within the individual. It is a time of great awakening. That means that what has happened to individuals has been a form of sleep, a form of fog, a form of sadness, a form of limitation, a form of harm. Those are forms. Those are constrictions. Those are created in order to learn, but the time for those limits is simply gone.

There is no other life beyond the life within. You will see that this is the moment of the great ascension.

You will see that the world is seeking that which it cannot find within the world. It is seeking justice, and peace, and joy—harmony, life. It is like the image that is projected on the mirror is not the harmony, justice, peace, life that is being sought. It is within the being and the image is only the image. The symbol is the expression of what exists therefore it is not found in the world. It is found within. The way is becoming clearer for living beings, at this point, to understand the projection on the mirror is not reality. It is only a symbol of reality. Reality is permanent and at peace and at one in harmony with the inner being and is indestructible.

It is a time of great awakening. There is no other life beyond the life within.

The Middle East problems stem, essentially, from the belief that it is destructible—that is can be destroyed, that it can be obliterated and there are means by which to obliterate life, for example, in the explosions and the atrocities. However, that does not obliterate life. That has not contained any of the life that exists and, therefore, whatever is projected is still not affecting the life within. The ascension involves understanding that which exists moving away from that which does not exist. It only exists, as an image.

The symbol is the expression of what exists therefore it is not found in the world. It is found within. The way is becoming clearer for living beings, at this point, to understand the projection on the mirror is not reality. It is only a symbol of reality.

It cannot be said enough that the image is only a visual image. It is a sensory image. It is a limited image. There is no image that can achieve the life within because it is a selection within a selection within a selection until it becomes an oversimplified picture of what exists. It is like trying to tell someone what you feel when you feel love. You cannot. It is a choice to place an image out there that expresses what is going on within. The love that is going on within can be expressed at the very best, minimally, through words, or poetry, or paintings, or whatever visual image can be achieved. It is still not the love within because the love within does not exist anywhere but truly within.

The prayer that goes on with the belief that life is destructible is important at this time. The prayer can be very specific in terms of allowing those who believe that life is destructible to understand life is indestructible, that to love is indestructible, that truth is indestructible, that there is nothing that can supersede those realities.

You will see that the image that is presented, for example, in the invention of television is only an image invented by the belief system of humanity and, therefore, what one sees on television is the truth, but the truth is not in the television set. It is not within those who present the information. It only exists within the individual being and that individual being does not exist within the projected image. It is important to understand the distinction at this point, because the prayer is not for the image. It is the prayer for the belief of destructibility. You will see what is occurring within is the enlargement of the understanding and of the love within. It is like the image of the being wandering in the desert. It is like seeking an answer within the environment rather than seeking an answer within. It is not necessary to wander. It is not necessary to seek without. It is not necessary to move without. It is not necessary to function without. It is only necessary to "enter into the closet and shut the door." It is only necessary to enter into prayer and as humanity reaches a point where its own belief systems have gotten to the point where it is simply fog, that the child is walking through the fog, humanity moves instantly into the light that exists within. It is not the creation of ascension. It is simply the movement that exists within.

You will see that there is much to be done in terms of the work of the many. It is not as the churches have taught. It is not like there is an "elect" and there is a "non-elect." Life does not function that way. Spring does not function that way. Love does not function that way. There are no limits.

You will see that life emerges as in spring blossoms. It is universal. It is comprehensive. That is the same with the ascension. The analogy is much closer to spring or to light or to love or to laughter or expression of that which exists within. It is not the imposition of the belief system on the mirror to that which exists within. That which exists within is being expressed without limit like sunlight, like peace, like abundance. When one thinks of the ascension, one must understand that it is abundance of light as never experienced before. It is coming out of a dark room into unlimited light. It is not that one is conscious of the coming out of the dark room into the unlimited light. It is just that it exists. It happens. It is there for all life. It is abundance beyond limits and nothing can stop it from happening. There is no fear of lack that can stop spring. There is no "sin," no sadness, no cruelty, no lack in any form that can stop spring from happening. It simply happens. When the time is right, it happens.

You will see that there is much that can be done within. There is much that can be done in accepting what exists within. There is much that can be done in allowing and relaxing and enjoying and praying and seeking and finding. That is what can be done. What cannot be done is to go to the mirror to solve the problems that exist upon the mirror because the mirror only reflects the belief systems of the individual. It is like water into a spring. If the fresh water comes into a puddle, the fresh water clears out the debris. It is much the same within.

When you become at one with your own being, you see that there is intrigue, fascination, and unlimited capacity to see the world in terms of its own true nature. It is looking on a beautiful field of flowers. The flowers all express the nature of the plant and yet there is variety and there is color and there is blossoming. It is varied and beautiful. But the destruction of the field is not varied. It is not beautiful. It is only the attempt to annihilate the living. It is not possible to annihilate the life of the plant. It is only possible to destroy the expression of the plant. This is a difficult concept for you to understand, but the existence of the plant comes from life itself. The destruction of the plant is only the attempt to stop life itself, but it does not destroy the plant. It only attempts to limit that particular plant, that particular place, that particular time. It is an impossible task to destroy all plants, in all time, in all places. It is impossible to annihilate life all times, all places. It is simply not possible, because the life of the plant exists. It is a reality. It is a certainty.

You will see that the great teachers have understood the nature of life and of metaphysical truth and of love and understood that the belief system that would see life as destroyed, was only a "system" of belief. It was only a creation of a being who saw the world "through the glass, darkly," who did not see the nature of reality.

The concept of Armageddon assumes that life is destructible. It is important to address that concept since the image on a mirror of the destruction that has been termed by the theologians as "Armageddon," as universal, is only limited to a given moment, at a given place, at a given time. When one understands that there is no time, that the image on the mirror is only an expression of the life that is underlying all reality, then one has to assume that Armageddon as projected by theology is not an accurate picture of what has been discussed in interpretation of Biblical literature. It is a different concept. You will see that the great teachers have understood the nature of life and of metaphysical truth and of love and understood that a belief system that would see life as destroyed, was only a "system" of belief. It was only a creation of a being who saw the world "through the glass, darkly," who did not see the nature of reality. "There is no fear in love." It is not the nature of love to do anything but be within itself and of itself and true to itself. It is how it exists. It is the nature of the individual being.

2

The Nature of the Present Time

THE PRESENCE

You will see that the nature of the present time is different from what you perceive it to be. You assume it is this minute and this minute and they are all the present time. It is not. It is this millisecond within a millisecond within a millisecond. It timeless. It is not the nature of time as you see it within your mind's eye and that is creating a great deal of difficulty in the perception of what is meant by the present so when one is "present" with someone, they are in the "presence" of someone. That is the nature of what is being discussed. So, that if you are in presence of love, you are at one with love. There is no time involved. If you are in the presence of a friend, you are with a friend at some level. It is not important that you think in terms of a moment with that friend. It is the presence of that friend. It is like when you are watching a sunset and the sunset is beautiful. You are no longer there. You are somehow involved with the sunset itself and the present time is like that. So when you are with what you are with, what you have termed "charity" or "kindness" or “goodness” or “justice” it is not that you are becoming a just person. It is that at that moment you are experiencing kindness or purity or justice and it is a different place than the place you typically are present. It is like when you are at the ocean and the wave hits your for just millisecond, you and the wave have become one and part of each other. It is not something that is planned. It is not something that is decided upon. It exists within itself. Your presence within yourself, like the child that is watching the flower, is your presence with your own being. It is not like, you will now watch the flower, and you will become present. It is not the same. Now, if that can be translated from a moment to the world. The world does not reach a point where it is “ascending.” It does not plan to ascend. It does not do good works in order to ascend. It does nothing but ascend. At the moment that the wave hits the individual, that is the moment at which humankind and all life ascends. It is not as you perceive it. The moment at which the ascension occurs is an endless perception of reality in which the individual is enmeshed within its own being. It is difficult to describe how much you are loved, how much

It is not like, you will now watch the flower, and you will become present. It is not the same. Now, if that can be translated from a moment to the world. The world does not reach a point where it is “ascending.” It does not plan to ascend. It does not do good works in order to ascend. It does nothing but ascend. At the moment that the wave hits the individual, that is the moment at which humankind and all life ascend.

your being is loved because when you describe love, you think in terms of time frames. You do not see the moment in which you are loved, not the moment in which you love. There is a difference.

You will see that there are many, many, many moments of complete ascension—complete ascension, that is, it is complete within itself and it is a very difficult concept to understand that it is not a moment in time in which the ascension occurs. It is within your own being that it actually occurs, so when we discuss the present time as you see it—it is a different perception of what "presence" is and within that presence, the ascension actually occurs. It does not actually occur in the world. It does not occur on the mirror. It does not occur in the visual picture of the world. It occurs within the heart. It occurs within the being of the individual. It is a transformation beyond any perceived transformation in the history of all life, anywhere. So when the great masters have spoken of the ascension, they have understood the nature of the ascension. You will see that there is a window within your own being that allows for that transformation. It is nothing you will do consciously. It will not be as you perceive it to be and it will be beyond all human comprehension.

One would have to be a quantum physicist and beyond to truly understand the nature of the present time with your language in order to use the language to translate the terms necessary.

You will see that there is much that you can do, humanly still. Your own experience is important to the entire process, but not the way you see it. You need to allow yourself time for mediation. You need to allow yourself time to wander and ponder and enjoy and experience. It is not as through you would like the luxury. It is important that you have those moments for yourself.

You will see that the present time is much, much more than you can possibly understand using language. That is why the meditation is a necessity when it comes to working with that understanding. It is much, much more than you can even imagine. One would have to be a quantum physicist, and beyond, to truly understand the nature of the present time with your language in order to use the language to translate the terms necessary. It is like the child that sees the sunset and knows the nature of the sunset, but cannot tell what the sunset actually does. It is like feeling, like a presence in the sunset itself. It is important for you to understand that when you experience something on this plane of existence, you are also experiencing it on many, many other planes of existence at the same time. It is not limited to this plane. It is not limited to your personality. It is not limited to your experience here on this plane of existence. It is much, much larger than you can imagine so that when you see a sunset, you see a broad spectrum of many, many levels of reality and were you to limit it to just this plane of existence, you would no longer be able to perceive what you perceive. The child sees the sunset and is in awe of the sunset because it is in awe of its own nature and its connection with what you have termed God, but it is not the God that is discussed in churches. It is the God that inspires and develops you as a being. That is within. And, that connection is not one that you are able to articulate because the words simply do not exist for that.

You will see that the churches have tried to discuss that and like the child that says, "I will now find joy in the sunset," the churches lose the joy within and the spontaneity within once they confine that experience to a given language or a given theology or a given paradigm. It is multifaceted and it literally moves to a thousand planes of existence in a given second.

You will see that the world is not reaching a point at which it simply moves to this other area of experience quickly. It moves with ease, without fear, without trepidation, without guilt, without sadness. It simply slips into it quickly and then remains there for longer, and longer periods of time as seen within this experience.

You will see that you can be gone for a second and that time is not relevant to that second. That is the nature of the present time.

The present time is like a window into the nature of reality. It is not like, "Ah, at this moment, I am in the present time." That is not the way it works. It is all there truly is. There is nothing but the present time. The illusion that exists that there is anything except the present time, except the nature of the individual, except the multiplicity of levels of understanding, except the beauty within, is the illusion that is leaving your experience.

The ascension involves the destruction of that perception of limits, of fear, of sadness, of unkindness. Those diminish until they are no longer perceived.

You will see that the minute that the child is hit by a wave, the child is at one with the wave. In much the same way, the adult that sees love for just a moment, sees their own nature, their own capacity. It is a state of consciousness that is unlimited. It is not one that is determined consciously. It simply happens within the individual. It is like laughter within that emerges to the outside experience. The journey as one laughs is a significant journey and, yet, it is perceived as a limited, short term thing within this perception of reality. It is, however, multidimensional as well.

The heart is barely been explored at this time, but the physicists and the intellectuals of this period will begin more and more to explore the nature of the heart itself. It is where the individual resides. It is the nature of the individual. It is the perception of the individual. It is the identity of the individual. It is what does not exist out there. It is what exists. It is like an enormous, enormous, unlimited room. It is without end. It is connected with the universe. It is connected with time beyond time. It is connected with all that there is and it exists within the nature of what is called the "present time." It is indestructible.

The heart is free of all fear.

The churches came in as a temporary solution to a created problem, but they are not the depth and breadth and wisdom of the heart.

You will see that the heart is not only the center of the individual. It is a window to the universe. It is difficult for you to understand at this point, that when one talks of space travel, or other ideas that they simply do not originate in the intellect. They come from a point of omniscience and that is the heart. It is almost as if blinders are put on consciously in order to limit the wisdom of the heart. It is like the individual seeks the limits in order to feel secure, but the wisdom is simply there and has always been there. It is indestructible. It is without limit and so that when one goes within, one solves problems. One sees visions. One understands their own being because it is the point at which they understand their own nature and connect with their own source. It is the Source of all life and all life reflects that source. That is why one can connect with another individual emotionally across the planet. It is omnipresent and omniscient. It is always present and all knowing.

When it comes to solving problems in the Middle East, for example, it is important to understand the solutions are not within the intellect. The solutions do not originate any place but what is termed the heart. It is felt. It is understood. It is intuited. It is free of limits. It is the only place any problem, anywhere, at any point was ever solved. It is available at all times. That is why, at this point, meditation is important, because one moves to that place of love, of peace, of joy, of understanding and does not have to live within the realm of superficial solutions to created problems. The world understands that at this point. The world is ready for its own affirmation of its own awareness at this point.

The churches came in as a temporary solution to a created problem, but they are not the depth and breadth and wisdom of the heart. They gain all of their power from the individuals that attend the churches, that come to the churches, that bring that power of the heart to the church itself. But the division that occurs within the churches at this point is destructive and limiting and, therefore, globally individuals are turning to meditation and prayer in order to heal the problems within the paradigm that is created. Underneath is reality. Underneath is the truth. Underneath is love. Underneath is primarily the understanding of the individual's capability of loving others, but the unlimited love that has created the individual to start with, the unlimited love that has created the earth, the unlimited love that has created life, the unlimited love that has created the beauty surrounding the individual. That is the nature of reality. That is the nature of truth. That is the nature of life itself.

The individual is not alone. The individual is at one and at peace.

You will see that the individual slides into that awareness, that is the moment that is termed the present time. The present time cannot be separated from God. The present time cannot be separated from individual. The present time has nothing to do with shorter concepts of what time is. The present time has only to do with life. It has only to do with the indestructible. It has only to do with the nature of reality.

The child is lost in the present. The child sees and experiences the present and the adult is a child who has chosen to live within the mirror and not relinquish the mirror.

The ascension and the nature of the present time are one.

You will see that the nature of the present time is an integral part of every life. It is not an exception to the life. It is the very nature of the life and, therefore, all life exists within the presence of its own being. That is the nature of "present time" because there is no time anywhere, at all, under any circumstances. Time is a fabrication. It is a deception. It is a creation so, within the presence of each being is a present time and the world projected on the mirror tries to call that a state of being that is reached once one leaves this plane of existence when it has nothing to do with leaving this plane of existence. It is this plane of existence and all planes of existence. The individual simply does not die. It is not easy to understand when one is living with a visual image and the visual image disappears. But, that is all that happens. The projected accumulation of beliefs about that individual disappears, but the individual has gone nowhere, has not changed in any way, and is present. The rationale for dealing with the image that is projected on the mirror is to say that the individual was born and then died and that is

That is the nature of "present time" because there is no time anywhere, at all, under any circumstances. Time is a fabrication. It is a deception.

the end of individual. But, the individual was never born. The individual never dies and their nature exists always on an unlimited level, so the illusion that that is the nature of the individual is vanishing, not the individual. The illusion is being destroyed, not the individual. The illusion is reaching an end, but not the individual. The illusion is facing, what the churches call Armageddon, but not the individual. The individual simply remains as it always has and always will, with no loss of continuity.

That is not hypothetical. It is the nature of what is real. It is the nature of the present. It is the nature of the presence. It is the nature of the individual. Now, in order to truly understand this, the individual only needs to enter a state of meditation. It connects them with their own being. The visual image of the individual simply disappears at that point. Did the individual cease to be? No. The individual remained during a state of prayer or a state of meditation, or the moment that the child is lost in the flower. The individual simply remained with no loss, with no limits, with no pain. The essence, the substance, the truth, the life, the soul of the entire being simply exists. It is in a state of being. The conscious mind comes in and out of that and plays like a seabird on the ocean. The ocean simply exists. The conscious mind comes and goes and darts, and creates, and recreates, and plays roles, and does a dance upon the nature of the individual. But, even within this plane of existence, the individual exists as the substance of the being that exists. When one loses a friend to what is called death, one does not lose a friend. The individual consciousness loses a conscious creation of who that friend actually was, but the individual simply remains.

So, the question remains what happens to the individual when they die? And the answer is absolutely nothing. Nothing happens. Nothing changes. Nothing falters. Nothing disappears. The consciousness if the individual seeking an answer to that question is confronting their own beliefs, their own systems into which they were born, their own understanding of the world, their own theories about what life is, but it does not change who that individual is. It does not change their presence. It does not change their capacity to do the same things that happen when they enter a state of meditation. It is all the same. The only existence that ever existed was the nature of the individual.

So you say that when the child is looking at the flower, that the child is alive, but child consciously disappears, so what happened to the child when they do not perceive themselves as here within this existence. They see themselves as part of the larger whole and they understand their own nature at that moment.

What you have termed existence is not what you see in each other, when you see the trees, the land, the sky the mountains, the life you perceive around you. You see that as existing. You see that as growing. You see that as being nurtured. You see that as life, but it is difficult for you to understand that a tree, for example, is frequently in a meditative state. It is in a connection with its own being. It is, what you term, "grounded." It is a being—an animal or any other being that you term life. It exists as its own being, but it does not exist as you see it exists, visually or with the senses. It exists without the senses. You understand this because you understand should you not be here, by your terms Is a being—an animal or any other being that you term life. It exists as its own being, but it does not exist as you see it exists, visually or with the senses.

It exists without the senses. You understand this because you understand should you not be here, by your terms, should you die, it still exists. It continues to exist whether or not your presence is here on this plane of existence and all this is a plane of existence. It is a segment of a segment of a segment of the whole. It is not the whole.

You see the world through the eyes you choose to see it through. It is not the entire picture and frequently you begin to see the larger picture and it is not easily articulated. It is difficult to communicate what the larger picture is all about. It is just that. It is the larger picture of the integrated whole. So you say that when the child is looking at the flower, that the child is alive, but child consciously disappears, so what happened to the child when they do not perceive themselves as here within this existence. They see themselves as part of the larger whole and they understand their own nature at that moment.

You will see that developments in art, music, physics—everything that you experience has come from the larger whole—is integrated into what you consciously project upon the mirror as reality and it is important for you to make that distinction at this time because you will see that the mirror will not house the individual any more. It is almost as if the individual has gained so much stature within their own conscious awareness of themselves that they cannot be contained within this plane of existence, of course they can, but it seems that that is the nature of the individual.

The ascension involves the at-one-ment with the presence of the individual so that the image on the mirror disappears ultimately. That diminished nothing. That takes away nothing. Nothing is lost. Nothing is removed. All that ever existed continues to exist. You will see that when the image on the mirror is removed, there is no death. There is no limit.

There is no right, no wrong, no good, no bad, no belief system differing from other belief systems. There is none of the need for utopias, community, fear, sadness. It is only the presence of the Presence within.

You will see that there is only joy. There is only peace. There is only truth. There is only understanding. The life you live begins to reflect that more and more as you live your life, it emerges. What changed? Nothing. You simply expressed that which exists within. You understood that which exists within. The change took place within your own being. It did not change externally. It is not as if there were an external event that changes how you let the prayer, the meditation, the understanding, the joy all emerge within your own experience. Was life diminished? No. Was it stopped? No. It simply emerged quickly to the light of love. It emerged quickly like the plant that grew quickly once the door was opened and the light flooded the room. Did it harm anything? No. It only expanded and expanded its own experience.

You will see that you are in the same place. You are in the same awareness. You are free of all fear at this point. You are transcending the world of fear so rapidly that you cannot keep up with your own growth. It is like a plant that is growing rapidly. It sees that it is growing rapidly in a sense. It only responds to the light, to the nurturing, to the joy, to the expansion that is going on within. It does not say, "I am growing." It simply grows.

Humanity is proceeding with the same kind of growth and all beings are involved—all life. It is difficult to imagine that it affects other forms of life as well, but it does. It affects the trees. It affects the plants. It affects the grass. It effects every life form there is, not only here, but in other places as well, so that as you grow, you are able to connect with others in other areas, in other dimensions, in other places, in other planets, in other spaces. It is difficult for you to understand the nature of cosmic time, of cosmic growth, of cosmic awareness. It is beyond your greatest imagination at this time, but it is very, very real. That is the nature of the ascension. Were life limited to this plane of existence, that would not be the case, because life would simply grow physically. That is not how life grows. It grows within. It expands within. It develops within it own being and the outward expression on this plane of existence begins to reflect some of it, but the bulk of it is reflected within the individual. Growth is the nature of the present time. It is the presence. It is growth within itself. You see the result of that when you see a plant grow from a small tree to a large being. It is within the nature of the tree to grow. It is within the nature of the tree to expand. It is within the nature of the tree to reach for the light. It is all within the tree. You have termed that DNA, but DNA is only an expression of nature of the individual tree. This is difficult for you to understand because then one assumes that all growth takes place on this plane of existence. It does not. This is only one plane of existence. You are functioning on literally thousands of planes of existence in any given second. The reason for the books coming into being is so that you will expand consciously as well as unconsciously and be aware of nature of the Presence of God, of your own unlimited nature within. It goes back to the concept that you must love, but you, truly, only love because it is your nature to love.

It is difficult for you to understand the nature of cosmic time, of cosmic growth, of cosmic awareness. It is beyond your greatest imagination at this time, but it is very real.

And it is more important for you to understand that you are loved, that you are blessed, that you are adored, that you are valued, that you are the beloved, that you are loved beyond anything that you can imagine. That is the door that is opening for you. The orthodox churches have tried to suppress that concept, but can no longer. The door that is opening is the door that obliterates the concept that you are a limited, simple mortal. You are not. You are the loved of love beyond your wildest imagination and the image on the mirror that projects that understanding is coming into being very rapidly. It is unstoppable. It is without limit. It will affect all life. It does affect all life.

So you see the world as the world. It is important that you see the image of the world. You visually see a planet, and then you visually see life on that planet, and then you see the individual life on that planet and you sense love. But love is the planet. Love is life on the planet. Love is the individual on the planet. It is all made up of nothing but love itself. It is difficult for you to understand that everything is made of the light of love. It is difficult for you to understand that the substance of all life is made up of what is termed within your language as love but that simply does not do the word justice. It is much broader than that. It is the kind of function that is understood by physicists, but it still remains within the realm of what you would term love. It is light slowed down to where it is visible. It is love slowed down to where it becomes

But love is the planet. Love is life on the planet. Love is the individual on the planet. It is all made up of nothing but love itself. It is difficult for you to understand that everything is made of the light of love.

language or person or sky or trees or mountains or whatever you experience. It is all still presence. It is all still the presence of what you have termed God. It is not separate from the individual. It is not something to be achieved. It is not something ethereal. It is the substance of all being. That is the line of demarcation with the truly orthodox concepts of what life is or God is. It is a different perception of being. That perception is facing its own being at this point. It is seeing itself as perception. It is seeing itself as the illusion of what is real.

You will use the light in many, many ways during the day. As living beings you utilize it all of the time. Physically you see that food source comes from light. You see that the earth depends on light. You see that you depend on light. But, you do not understand that that is from within, not from without. That dependency on light is within your own being. It is part of your being. It is integrated into your being. It is not from without. It is truly from within so that when you eat a plant that has utilized the light to create its own leaves, and you consume the plant to maintain your life on this plane of existence, it is symbolic, truly, of the nature of being. Many, many enlightened beings have tried to explain this phenomenon, but the world simply was not ready for it. It did not see it. It did not understand it. It needed so very much to retreat into its own perception of its own perception. It was never its understanding of what was true, or permanent, or the nature of the individual, and yet you still understand the nature of the individual. You do, on some level, always, no matter how dark the room seems, you still understand that your nature is not the reactions of light. Your nature is light, itself.

You will see that you are not what you think. It will become very clear in the near future. You are much, much more than you can even try to imagine What you are doing on the human level is to synthesize so much of what goes on elsewhere within your own consciousness. It is not easy for you to stay here on this level all of the time because it is not an easy place to spend a great deal of your being. So, many, many more are using meditation to connect with the other plane of being and then return to this plane. It is not unusual for you to break from this plane on a momentary basis as well as a longer-term basis as happens with meditation. It is very easy for you, for example, to look at a scene and then return rather instantly within a time frame. But, what happens within that time frame is that you travel within your own being. That is timeless.

It is very easy for you, for example, to look at a scene and then return rather instantly within a time frame. But, what happens within that time frame is that you travel within your own being. That is timeless.

The sense that you have of what time is, is incorrect at best. Time is not a sequence. Time is a movement, for example, when you see a beautiful flower, observe it, and return, you are not sure how long you were basically gone. You have gone somewhere. You know. But, it is not easy for you to determine how long that actually took. That is similar to those who say they have been abducted by aliens and then said time was of no relevance. That is true because other dimensions have frequently understood and mastered time. It is easier than you think to leave this plane of existence and then return. For example, you spend what you call time in sleep, but that is not as you see it. Sleep is a moment. It is not eight hours. It is a moment within the cosmic realm and what this book is talking about is the nature of time within the multiple dimensions on which you function, so time is of importance to you in terms of linear sequences and you assume that there is eight hours sleep when there is an entire experience in what you call each night.

Children know this and utilize this time extremely well. Sometimes they, also because of their introduction to the world of fear, are also are bound by the world of fear during the night time, because they are so very close to what you have termed, and the books have termed, the world of love that there is such a juxtaposition for them, that they do not quite understand the movement to and from the two dimensions. It is an adjustment for them and, therefore, they have, what you call, nightmares because it is such a huge adjustment for them. In time, according to your sense of time, they can make that adjustment and can move more easily from this dimension to the dimension from which they truly function. They are the renewal for this dimension. They are the projection of their being on the mirror to show you that the mirror is not all there is.

It is critical for you to understand that the mirror is not all there is now because the mirror is losing it charm for you and your need is to return more and more to your home, to your consciousness, to your being, to your soul, to your self, and to the love that binds you with all life. It is present all of the time, everywhere, anywhere you look on this planet. That love is there and binds all life to all life. It is nothing that is new. It is nothing that is discovered. It exists. So when you think in terms

It is critical for you to understand that the mirror is not all there is now because the mirror is losing it charm for you and your need is to return more and more to your home, to your consciousness, to your being, to your soul, to yourself, and to the love that binds you with all life.

of time, you must not think in terms of linear sequence. You must not think in terms of birth/death, birth/death, birth/death but, rather, in terms of multi-dimensional learning, multi-dimensional understanding, multi-dimensional living.

You will see that there is much to be understood and what happens now is that, collectively, you have emerged from what is known as the "world of fear." It is enormous. The shift in consciousness is so great that like the child that is adjusting to the world of fear, you are adjusting now to the world of love. You are now adjusting to the ascension. You are now adjusting to freedom from fear. It is like explosion of the heart that is bursting forth. It is like nothing that has ever happened before in the "human" experience. It does not exist in your so-called, history.

The world is, in a sense, vanishing, but the vision of the world vanishing is not what you think it is. The world is simply shifting. The world is becoming free. The world is becoming joyous. The world is becoming non-combative, non-argumentative, not afraid. You will see that there is much to learn on each dimension now so that is another reason to not spend a great deal of time here, because there is so much to learn at so many levels that it is difficult for you to stay here and at this level learn only at this level. It is not enough for you. It will not satisfy your needs right now. And, therefore, what you do is you leave more frequently. You travel more frequently to other dimensions and spend your time learning at all kinds of levels as this is a tremendous growth period as life as part of the whole. As the salt in the stew is part of the stew, you are a part of this huge learning experience that is not seen visually. It is not seen upon a mirror. It is within your being and will emerge to the mirror as you develop within one multi-level learning. You must not worry about each other because each of you is learning as you must. There are no more standards for the right way to live because what is happening in your life, is happening at so many levels, that it is not a stereotypic kind of experience for an unlimited, loving, multi-dimensional being. It cannot be contained within this dimension. It has superseded this dimension in so many ways that you can no longer define what your life is here because it is so many things that emerge from so many different levels.

You will see that there is much to understand quickly. You will see that there is actual physical presence with thoughts. Thoughts are not as you perceive, ethereal in nature. They actually have a presence of their own and they exist within your own being so that you can think of something and it, essentially., takes up residence within your being. That is not limited to you or anyone else. It has an existence as well. When you think a loving thought towards someone that becomes part of your being. It is not the same as becoming part of your experience so that when you love someone, you experience love with the other person. But the true, existing love within your being goes on and has always existed and will always exist. When you think of this, you think of soul mates and those you love in your life. They, in fact, exist within your being as well. It is like recognizing something outside that exists within you, and, therefore, you love them for what already exists within your own being. Then you share an experience with another individual and you call that love.

Time is a fabrication within this plane of existence and it simply cannot connect to the multiple planes of existence in which you actually function and, therefore, it is very difficult for you to hold on to time because it is not part of what you truly experience.

But the love that exists is within you and the connection with the other individual is within you and the love you experience is within you and the life you experience is within you. And they exist within you and you exist within them, and, therefore, you have that connection because of the nature of your being, not because you somehow met on another plane and the experience on the mirror, and that was what existed, that love. It is like being alone with yourself, but with the world at the same time.

You will see that time simply does not exist. It is nonexistent. When you adjust to concept, you will begin to understand the nature of reality. Reality does not exist as a linear sequence. That is the way it is. Linear sequences are the image on the mirror. They do not exist within your being and they are losing their hold on your experience because you have become closer and closer to your nature as a spiritual being. Time is a fabrication within this plane of existence and it simply cannot connect to the multiple planes of existence in which you actually function and, therefore, it is very difficult for you to hold on to time because it is not part of what you truly experience. It is like saying to yourself, "I will hold on to the concepts that 2+2 =5. It is hard for you to hold on to it because it is not true to your nature. It is not true to your understanding of reality. It is not true to who you are. It is not true. So, time is an untruth that you are attempting to hold on to and it will leave very quickly because what you are truly dealing with is within your nature. It is within cosmic time. It is within the nature of nature itself. It has not been 2000 years since Jesus came to this experience here that you frequently discuss. It is within.

It has not been 2000 years since Jesus came to this experience here that you frequently discuss. It is within.

When you relinquish the concept of time, and the concept of generations, and the concept of history, and the concept of anything but the nature of your being, then you understand many of the Biblical teachings as spiritual teachings across this experience and that is that there is no time and, therefore, when Christians say that Jesus is here as a "second coming", in fact, there was never any experience in which that did not occur, because there was no time. The hardest adjustment, conceptually, that you will deal with within the next period of time, according to your belief system, is the concept that there is no time. When you talk in terms of the present time, when you talk of the "second coming", when you talk of the ascension, it all exists, simply, within the present time. It exists nowhere else. It is within the presence of the Presence and there, truly, is nothing else. And the churches teach that there was a period of time in which there was a great master and then 2000 years later that master will appear and there will be a "second coming" and there will be the ascension. Know all things will happen, but that is not the nature of the Presence.

The only true place in which you can understand this is in the area of meditation because at that point you are connected with your larger being and that gives you the understanding that you need to understand a concept as immense as that concept is. When you see others beginning to grasp this concept then you will delight in the sharing of that understanding. It is like a snowball. It will grow quickly.

The way is becoming very clear for the world to see the nature of the present time, the Presence, the unchanging, the permanent nature of presence. The world is fleeting because it is fleeting. It is not permanent. It is not constant. It is not substantial. It is not filled with understanding of its own being. It assumes its own being from what is seen visually of what is the image, what is the projected image upon the mirror and says that is permanent when that is not the nature of the present time. The nature of present time is much like the image of the mountain. It is substantial. It is cohesive. It is life supporting. It is large. It appears permanent. It is not as permanent as one assumes, but it is an image of what one thinks of when one thinks of the nature of the Presence within each individual. To understand the present time, one must enter within, one must meditate, one must seek all answers from within the being and not from without. The answers do not exist without. They only exist within. The world is in a difficult time, not because of what is going on within the individual because what is going on within the individual is peace, is joy, is love, is truly where the ascension takes place. What is happening in the world at this point is the projection on the mirror as discontinuity, is disassociated with what is going on within each individual and, therefore, seems not to reflect that which is happening within. In fact, it is reaching a point at which it will have more and more discontinuity until, at last, it takes a serious look at what is happening. It does not change because it looks at what is happening, though. It changes because, from within, that new order, that beauty, that love, that joy is all occurring within and will create the image on the mirror. It is what the Christians seek in their belief systems, but it does not exist within the belief systems. It exists within each individual.

The way is becoming very clear for the world to see the nature of the present time, the Presence, the unchanging, the permanent nature of presence.

It is like when one is going through a difficult time and one is praying for help. In fact, the help arrives in some form and the individual gets through the difficult time. The area of the Middle East in which difficulty is occurring is still a projected area upon the mirror of human experience. It is not the truth of each individual in the Middle East, in the United States, within every part of the world. It is only within the image upon the mirror. It is important that individuals pray, that they meditate, that they seek answers and that they understand that this is occurring because as the freedom the limits occur, the image upon the mirror begins to alter itself. One assumes, for example, with an election that one tried. That is not the case. That was an image that was created long, long ago. That has nothing to do with what is going on within at this point. That is the discountenance. That is the difference between what is within and what is without and universally that is difficult for all beings, for all life, not just human life at this point. It is important to understand that the life that you experience is connected to all other life and that continuum is the permanent nature of the presence, of the timelessness of the peace, of the joy, of the love that, in Biblical terms, "... passes all understanding, " that permeated everything.

You will see that there will be a time of what human beings have called "pain," of sorrow, of suffering, of difficulty.

3

The Nature of Love

The world of love is within the present, is always here, is within the heart, is within the being of each individual. It is not separate from the being. It is difficult to envision what this actually means. It means that when one enters into the world of love, one enters into a permanent part of the nature of your own being. It is like you go into a home that you love. It is comfortable. It is at peace. It is joyous. It is at one with your own being. It is loving. It is not fearsome like being out in a storm or being in a fearful situation. It is within.

It is difficult to imagine what the present time truly means in conjunction with what has been termed the world of love. For example, if you were a child and you were playing within your own home and you felt comforted and at peace and at one with yourself without any

You cannot discuss the present time without discussing what love is. They are tied completely to each other.

threat, you would be within that place. Did you ever leave that place? No, you did not. It is within your own being. And so, humanity is at a crossroads where it actually can envision what it is like to come home, what it is like to leave the storm, what it is like to leave the war, what it is like to leave the conflict, what it is like to leave such fear that it overwhelms the individual that it creates such sadness that does not seem to leave in a lifetime. All of those things are part of what is termed "a world of fear." You truly believe still that it is part of an evolution. It is not. The greatest fallacy within the thinking of the individual at this point is that it takes time to get to the point to where one is "home." It takes no time. Time does not exist. If you really understand the present time, you understand that all of that exists within. It is not exterior to your being. It does not take time to achieve it. It does not take great social movements or anything but the understanding that it exists within. It is like assuming that in order to get to the shore, when one is standing on the shore, it takes swimming out into the ocean and coming back. One simply stands on the shore. One simply understands the nature of the present time. One simply understands that they never left the shore, that the shore was always there, and that they were always standing on the shore.

The joy that comes from that understanding, can overwhelm the individual, and, yet, it is as though you need to project on the mirror other things still, but without accepting what exists within. The mirror exists without. The tribulation exists without. The politics exists without. The lack exists without, but it does not exist within and when one truly understands the present time, one understands the love that goes on is unlimited. It is joy without any limit, without any bound, without anything but its own being.

The world is an arena in which the forces, in effect, are forces that clash sometimes because of the nature of the belief systems that have evolved over, what you term, a long period of time, but, actually, they evolved within each individual who subscribe to those belief systems. The world does not distinguish between these systems of belief. It assumes that they are the truth and they do not understand that they are simply systems of belief that evolved in what you call a long period of time. They actually did not evolve the way you perceive it. They actually evolved within the soul, the being, the nature of each individual and as the individual enters what is called the world of fear, the individual then chooses to subscribe to a given belief. The belief, then, has much control over much of the activity of the individual as the individual seeks to remain true to the tenants of whatever belief it is.

The world is an arena in which the forces, in effect, are forces that clash sometimes because of the nature of the belief systems that have evolved over, what you term, a long period of time, but, actually, they evolved within each individual who subscribe to those belief systems.

The individual tries not to differ with that belief system, but, rather, to prove what they understand within themselves to be true is expressed without. It is like the image on the mirror attempts to be a purer image on the mirror rather than to reflect what exists within each individual. The purity of the mirror is not the same as the purity within the individual. The system is limited. All belief systems are simply limited ways of looking at the nature of being. They are not as expansive as the nature of each individual, and, therefore, the conflict exists within the individual. Imagine a loving being who truly loves all and then is told that their group is simply more important than the next group. That creates a conflict within each individual. That conflict is then expressed in the outward world, but that does not alter the nature of the individual, nor does it alter the nature of the love in which the individual exists.

As love expands within the individual, like the plant growing in sunshine, it supersedes the mirror. It supersedes the belief system. It supersedes whatever one does to try to be moral by be being more moral than what is projected to be the correct way to exist. It is like a child laughing in the sunshine. The child does not laugh because it is trying to be good. The child laughs because the sunshine is beautiful and the sunshine is pouring upon the child and it all blends within the individual. That laughter is the nature of the individual. The desire to follow a given moral code is not within the nature of the individual. It is within the projection on the mirror.

The heart is where it takes place. It is difficult to understand that the intellectual systems have had their day. They have had their following. They have had their power. They have had their say. They simply are not the nature of each individual and like a beautiful stream pouring out of a mountain, the nature of the individual, simply, is coming to the fore at this point. And, when that happens, the wars ultimately cease. The conflicts ultimately cease. The fear subsides to the point where it no longer has control over individuals. You will see this very soon within your own world as you perceive it, for that is all that exists is perception and you will find that no matter what you do, it will take place without in your world. It is a hopeful thing, but it is only because it is time for the hopeful. It is time for the ascension. It is time for the tremendous growth that occurs within each individual. It is taking place within before it ever occurs without.

You love. You love beyond your greatest imagination. And each individual loves and they love beyond their greatest imagination.

There is a paradigm that humanity has functioned within. The world of fear is what it is called, but it is an entire paradigm. It is an assumption of death. It is an assumption of pain. It is an assumption of suffering. It is an assumption of what the theologians call "the cross." It is an assumption that that is real, that it is not a creation. But, in fact, it is a creation. It is a paradigm created to learn from, but it is no longer the framework from which you function. When you move beyond that paradigm, you simply more beyond the paradigm. You have left it behind. It is not yours anymore.

The way that one envisions the ascension is becoming clearer, is becoming obvious to many in so many ways. It is like learning to walk. Once the child has learned how to walk, they know how to walk and they begin to explore the areas that walking takes them. They become mobilized. They become able to move to other areas as well. Until the child could walk, the child was not in a position where they could go, what they could do. As you become more and more aware of the areas available to you, you become willing to move to those areas. It is very much like learning to ski, or swim, or fly an airplane, or anything else that you learn to do that allows you to move beyond where you are. Suddenly, the world becomes available and that is true with that world of love. Suddenly, the world of love becomes more and more available to the individual and they wish to explore those areas because they understand those areas they understand that they no longer have to crawl in order to achieve a given goal.

The way is becoming available for humanity as well. There is a paradigm that humanity has functioned within. The "world of fear" is what it is called, but it is an entire paradigm. It is an assumption of death. It is an assumption of pain. It is an assumption of suffering. It is an assumption of what the theologians call "the cross." It is an assumption that that is real, that it is not a creation. But, in fact, it is a creation. It is a paradigm created to learn from, but it is no longer the framework from which you function. When you move beyond that paradigm, you simply more beyond the paradigm. You have left it behind. It is not yours anymore.

All life is moving beyond a death, generational, fear based paradigm. It is no longer within the head. It is within the heart. It is difficult for you to imagine a world you know now, free of fear. It is a challenge for you at this time.

A world free of fear is one that you understand that there is no death, that you simply never die, that you were never born and you never die. What you assume about birth and about death is that you came here and that you will die. That is only entering into a paradigm. That is not who you are. That is the single most radical change that takes place when one moves from the "world of fear" to the "world of love". It is like telling a kindergartner that they do not know now how to color or to walk or to sing songs or whatever they enjoy, that they are still a baby. They are not. They have grown. They have learned. They have progressed. They have developed and they no longer belong to the realm of babyhood with its limits. They were loving. They were kind. They were smart.

They were good, but they are not limited to do what they were capable of. You are now capable of feeling. You are now capable of loving. You are now capable of expanding beyond your wildest imagination. That is what is happening within.

Then the question arises, "What happens when wars continue, and fear continues, and hate seems to continue?" You will see that it continues only upon the mirror. It continues only within the paradigm. It continues only within a limited consciousness. It does not continue, in fact. It is important for you to understand the distinction between the two at this point, because you have grown so rapidly, so recently, so completely, that you can no longer cling to the image upon the mirror. It remains only an image. When healing actually occurs within the individual, it miraculously appears upon the mirror. It miraculously appears out there, but the healing that actually occurred, occurred within the individual. That is true for humanity. When the healing occurs miraculously for humanity, it does not occur on the mirror. It occurs within each individual. The way is occurring. The way is becoming so very clear to you at this point collectively. When you truly understand the nature of love, you understand all things: the mirror and the being. It is like the image upon the mirror could not exist without the light within. When you discuss "energy," you discuss the light within. When you discuss changes, physically, you understand that it is the impact of the light within, upon the image, upon the mirror, but the light within exists within the light within. The image upon the mirror has no life. The image upon the mirror has no truth. The image upon the mirror has no existence. It is only a reflection of the existence within. It is only a reflection of the individuality within. It is only a reflection of the life within. It is life expressed, but the life exists within.

It is a time of tremendous growth for humanity. It is such a welcomed time within the heart.

You are used to a separate image visually, for you assume that the visual picture is the true picture. It is not, because there is this interplay among all beings on a global scale and what is happening within the consciousness of each individual, it the global scale is moving to a cosmic scale.

You will see that the world being collectively, develops its own path collectively, as well, so that when you join with others as the salt in the stew. You are immersed within the collective paths. That is different from the image on the mirror. That is the collective awareness within all life. That is within the individual, but it is within the individuals collectively, so that as life emerges from what is called the world of fear, it emerges collectively as well. It means, that, and this has been said many times, all animals, and plants, and life, as a whole emerges. It, actually, becomes more beautiful. It becomes more enlarged. It becomes filled will largess. It becomes more loving collectively. It becomes more aware, collectively, of the nature of reality. Collectively emerges. That is part of the entire nature of the planet. The planet emerges collectively, as well. It is a life support system collectively because it is life collectively. It is an important issue for you to understand, because as you love, the planet loves. The earth loves. The plants love. The animals love and it is not divorced from their nature of love. The planet actually becomes a more friendly place because collectively, it is more at peace with its own being. There is no life that is separated from all life, and, yet, within that life, there is individuality.

It is hard for you to envision this because you are used to the visual image and the image upon the mirror, but you have a sense of what that is because, collectively, you understand it. That is how you are able to communicate with other forms of life. That is how you are able to lean against a tree and feel the love that's within the tree, because you are all part of the collective awareness as well as the individual awareness. It is how people enjoy pets, how they enjoy animals, how they enjoy plants, how they enjoy growing things. It is how they enjoy nurturing all life, because all life is collectively a part of all life. You are used to a separate image visually, for you assume that the visual picture is the true picture. It is not, because there is this interplay among all beings on a global scale and what is happening within the consciousness of each individual, it the global scale is moving to a cosmic scale. It is hard to envision this yet, but some have begun to understand the nature of this movement within the individual and within the collective awareness. It is beyond your greatest imagination. It is beyond your greatest science. It is beyond your greatest understanding, except that you do understand it within the heart. You feel it within the heart. You understand its unlimited nature because within the heart is where it exists and it is unlimited.

That expansion that is taking place makes the planet more healthy, makes the planet more beautiful, makes all life more at peace. The Biblical teachings were to attempt to envision something that could not be envisioned at that point. It is like the child that is learning to walk. The child that is learning to walk simply does not understand what it is like to run a marathon but attempts to envision what that actually is. And as they train and begin to work out, and begin to learn to run, and begin to learn to run more quickly, and begin to do all of the things that eventually lead up to a marathon, then the child sees clearly what the marathon entails. The child may not have had the clear vision, but the child learns the clear vision. And so, some of the prophecies are the largest that could be imagined and never lost their validity because they were on the correct path. They simply were not able to quite envision what the entire picture assumed. It is time of rejoicing. It is a time of great joy. It is a time of a collective joy. It is joy for the earth. It is joy for the planet. It is Joy for the cosmos and beyond. It is not limited.

The experience of many is permeating the collective awareness. The experience of many is permeating thought, is permeating life, is affecting the entire picture. It is a hopeful thing. It is a loving thing. It is a peaceful thing. It is specific to the individual, but still part of the whole.

You will see that the way is becoming more and more clear to you as the world removes itself further and further from your soul's purpose. It is important that you understand that the way is clear. It is without blemish. It is spotless. It is free of the fears, the eons of pain, the suffering, the brutal actions of individuals on this plane of existence. It is like a clean slate. It is like a crystal way in light of the darkness that has occurred within thought. It is only within belief. It is only within thought. It is only the image on the mirror. It is not the nature of the individual to have committed atrocities, and, therefore, it is important for you to understand that the second

"Ultimately, you will see what is mean by the 'present time.' It is not where events occur. One assumes that his event is occurring in the present time, right now. It is not. What you see and what you experience as an image is what has occurred, because to truly be in the present time, you do not exist within the image."

coming occurs within each individual, it occurs universally. It occurs within each individual. It occurs within each individual—the crystal within them, the purity within them, the love within them, is all that becomes real. The atrocities, the fear, the anger, the pain ceases to be experienced—ceases to be real because it was, in fact, an image. It was, in fact, a belief. It was, in fact, a fear.

Imagine leaving a fearful, fearful room to emerge to a beautiful garden in which no fear existed. That is essentially what happens within consciousness, but it occurs on a level that is not a conscious level so as these experiences shift, the individual shifts and it is like moving on from kindergarten to the first grade. You simply don't think a great deal about what you learned in kindergarten, you simply focus on the present time, the nature of the present time.

Ultimately, you will see what is mean by the "present time." It is not where events occur. One assumes that his event is occurring in the present time, right now. It is not. What you see and what you experience as an image is what has occurred, because to truly be in the present time, you do not exist within the image. You actually exist within that millisecond of the present and it like opening a door to awareness, you simply did not understand clearly prior to arriving at that awareness. The experience that you have that you call the present time is truly the past. It is no longer present. When you love completely, when the moment the child is lost in the flower, the moment of "Aha!," the moment you are hit by the wave—all those are within the present—the Presence of the individual, the love of the individual, the metaphysical truths of the individual. Those are what exist. That is existence. The image is simply manipulating the past in some form and some way that is acceptable to the individual. That is the belief system. That is what is projected on the mirror. That is what we seem to experience here on this plane of existence. That is why the conflicts are irreconcilable, because they have no life to them. They no longer, truly, exist. The only moment they had life was the moment in which they were occurring within the present time—within the Presence. So the conflict that is occurring is within remembrances within belief, is within the world of fear, is within the perception of each individual and perception is not the same for every individual because there are so many belief systems involved, plus fears, and anxieties, and deliberate misconceptions, and non deliberate misconceptions. This complicated thing that you call "reality" is much more complicated than you can even imagine, but it is still only the perception of reality. The reality, the life, the truth, the soul, the mind, the spirit, the love, the being is all within the Presence. That is like the spring from which everything comes. It is the nurturing. It is the beauty. It is the awareness. It is the substance of the individual.

You will see that what theologians have called the "Presence of God" is the only existence there is. It is not that God is in our lives. It is that Presence is within the individual. It is like when they have spoken of the Son of God—it is like the presence of the Presence in the nature of the individual. It is universal. It is universal to all life. It is not just human life. The nature of love, the nature of joy, the nature of life is universal to all life. It seems obvious to say that, but it is does not seem obvious to the individual belief systems. The way is becoming clear for you

"It is not that God is *IN* our lives. It is that Presence is within the individual. It is like when they have spoken of the Son of God—it is like the presence of the Presence in the nature of the individual. It is universal."

to be able to articulate the power of just that reality. When you truly understand that all life is of God, in God, through God, about God—all life becomes sacred, becomes beautiful, becomes loving, becomes life-giving, becomes truth telling, becomes real to each individual. As the belief systems begin to fade away, the fear based belief system, the universality of all life becomes more and more obvious to individuals. It is not a contrived thing like saying, "I should be aware that all life is of God." It is sacred. It is the understanding that it is the case, therefore, one does not proselytize. It is like enjoyment. It is like laughter. It is occurring and it does not have to be explained ad naseum. It needs to be experienced.

Life itself is church, religion, truth, all of the things that have been categorized into the realm of what is called theology, but, in fact, is so much more universal, that it is impossible to confine it to those areas of thought. It becomes more and more contrived, the more the individual attempts to limit the understanding of the nature of God. It is not liberal. It is not conservative. It is not restrictive. It is the nature of breath. It is the nature of life. It is nature of reality. It is the nature of nature. The issue then becomes what happens to individuals when they cease to exist within this plane of existence? It becomes critical, at that point, for individuals to understand because as they see the world, it is crumbling so they must know that there is something else beyond what they perceive to be true.

The churches were not able to hold on to the truth because they had to work on the image within the mirror. It is not possible to have the image of the mirror pure, clear, clean, crystal as it is within the present time. It is simply an impossibility and, therefore, they gave themselves an impossible task. They attempted to create, within the image on the mirror, what existed within the individual and it cannot be done. It is impossible.

You will see that the way is becoming easier for all life. It is like sliding down a beautiful stream in the sunlight. It becomes easier as you go. You simply become more lost in the present. You become more enthralled by the experience. You become more at peace with yourself and the life around you. It is easier for you to understand that when you leave this plane of existence, that it is like leaving a room. It is nothing more. You have never changed. The life you live has never changed. The expression of that life has never changed. You left the room, but it is of no consequence as far as the life that is your being. The room that you have left is the image on the mirror, is the memory of the image within the mirror. It is the memory of what you experienced within the present time within the room. You will not be afraid of death. You will not be concerned about death. The world of fear is concerned and absorbed with death. But as you leave the world of fear, you no longer care about death It does not absorb you. It does not control you. It does not govern your being.

You are a being of light. You are a being of love. That light, that love does not change. It is more permanent than a rock. It is more permanent than the longest lives of trees. It is more permanent than the stones upon the earth. It is within its own nature, unlimited and permanent. When you finally see this, the world transforms itself.

You are a being of light. You are a being of love. That light, that love does not change. It is more permanent than a rock. It is more permanent than the longest lives of trees. It is more permanent than the stones upon the earth. It is within its own nature, unlimited and permanent. When you finally see this, the world transforms itself.

4

THE NATURE OF TRUTH

You will move on to the next category, which is the nature of truth itself. It is a difficult term for you because you have sought it within the image on the mirror and it is the substantial part of your identity. It is of great importance to the nature of your nature. It is, without a doubt, the most important lesson learned on this plane of existence and it is a lesson for all life. One assumes that it is, without a doubt, the most important lesson learned on this plane of existence. It is a lesson for all life. One assumes that it is not true for the plants, or the rocks, or the trees, or the grasses, or the bushes, or the animals, or the other forms of life do not deal with truth, but they do within the form

It is an honesty within that allows an individual to look directly into the light, to reflect the light, to play in the light, to absorb the light, to be at one with the light without having to return to the darkness.

that they have chosen. They have a chosen a form for a reason for them. It is a kingdom within a kingdom. The truth of a predator is blatant truth. It is dealing with the killing of life in order to remain life. It is very complex for that being. It is gross. It is true. It is true for that life, but what is happening within the world of fear is that the predators are leaving this plane of existence because fear is vanishing as a lesson for life.

The concept of war is a complicated concept and it is the clash of concepts. It is the clash of ideas. It is the clash of belief systems. It is the clash of fear based belief systems, so that when the individual begins to ascend, it is not that wars begin to cease. It is that the clash between those who hold beliefs dear to their hearts, begin to encounter conflict less and less. It is important that prayer occur universally to ease this process. It is difficult for you to understand that the actual prayer affects the events of the individuals, but it does. There is a truth to war. There is a historic truth to war. There is a historic truth to understanding the enemy. The great masters have understood this and said that the enemy was frequently the individual's greatest friend, because the individual had to face the enemy within and it, like those entire systems, those armies those legions vanish into thin air as thought emerges from the world of fear. It is like the world decides universally to drop the mantle of fear, to drop the burden, to drop the pain, to drop the atrocities, to drop the inhumanity, to drop the burden of its own fear and to rise into its own nature. It will astound you as this happens, but within your own being you understand that that is exactly what is happening and so you are not as in awe of it and as involved in it as you have been. You will see that the image on the mirror is beginning to lose its color. It is losing its form. It's losing its hold. What is happening is within each individual, the excitement of going within, of prayer, of manifesting is becoming more and more intriguing. It is the individual seeking the truth within, not without. It is an honesty within that allows an individual to look directly into the light, to reflect the light, to play in the light, to absorb the light, to be at one with the light without having to return to the darkness.

You will see that the world is a complicated arena in which it is almost as if the molecules of thought are bombarding each other in a complex pattern. The dance that occurs is one in which the individuals seek to resolve their relationships with themselves and those exterior to themselves. It is difficult to understand that that is like the molecules within a chair or within a stew oar within a complete structure, but, in a sense, that is what is happening and the formation that is created is the earth, of its ancillary parts, of all the interactions that exist within this remarkable sphere that is residence of life itself. You will eventually understand the nature of the core of this remarkable earth as well. It is not limited to the earth, however, it is the microcosm within the macrocosm that exists universally and it is difficult to understand that that is still only one plane of existence. That which you term life is universal. The ascension occurs within universal life. It occurs within the moment of truth. It

That is what happens to life itself when you leave this plane of existence. It is of no significance. It is crystalline in form and that life remains. That does not alter in any way so that whatever happens to the life here, on this plane of existence, it remains in its crystalline form. It is true. It is free of anything that is done to it.

occurs, truly, within a moment of the most simple of forms and that is the truth itself. It occurs within the millisecond of being so that the earth is shifting as well as the individual lives as well as thought as well as each level of completion of the work of the component parts of the whole. The truth exists as an idea. It is crystalline in form. It can be lied about. It can be disfigured. It can be altered, but it remains in its crystalline form. That is what happens to life itself when you leave this plane of existence. It is of no significance. It is crystalline in form and that life remains. That does not alter in any way. So that whatever happens to the life here, on this plane of existence, it remains in its crystalline form. It is true. It is free of anything that is done to it. It is free of any abuse. It is free of any alteration. It is free of any pain. It simply remains the truth. If one were to add 2+2=5, it does not alter the truth that 2+2=4. It cannot be altered within its own being. It is true to its own being at all points. That is true of love. That is a different aspect of the same whole. It does not matter that 2+2=4 has been altered, changed, lied about. It remains true to what it is. So that is true with individuals as well. Their nature remains true to what it is.

Healing occurs as that truth remains within the individual experience. The image on the mirror is altered by the image of the truth. It is like if one were to try to misrepresent the truth and add a huge column of figures incorrectly, it still would be corrected by adding them correctly. It is of no consequence that the entire column of figures was added incorrectly. All that matters, is that column was added at some point. Breakthroughs within physics and science and theology and music occur as the crystalline form appears reflected upon the mirror. But the crystalline form exists within first, and then is reflected upon the mirror, is projected. It affects the entire picture upon the mirror. It releases the picture to its own nature.

You will see that the truth is much, much more simple than you even see. It is like a straight line. It is like a prairie without a sky. It is a simple thing. It is not intricate and complicated. You will understand the nature of timeless truth. It is not within the image, however. You understand that language is an image as well and it does not exist within language. It does not exist within the mirror. It exists within the individual. It does not contain time. It has no boundaries. It has no measured out sequence. It exists in and of itself as a simple, powerful reality. The reality of truth is not abstract. It is very real. It is very specific. It is very enlightened. It is unencumbered. That which is true is not bound in any dimension, in any life form, in any place. That which is true exists in and of itself without any kind of physical, mental, spiritual boundaries. It is accessible at all times because it exists without time. That which is true is that which is freeing humanity. It is as if the image on the mirror became encumbered, became bound, became constricted by the actions of the individuals. There was an assumption, like covering a light that it could

The reality of truth is not abstract. It is very real. It is very specific. It is very enlightened. It is unencumbered. That which is true is not bound in any dimension, in any life form, in any place. That which is true exists in and of itself without any kind of physical, mental, spiritual boundaries. It is accessible at all times because it exists without time. That which is true is that which is freeing humanity.

be limited. It could not. The light is free. It is not limited by those who attempt to cover it, or limit it. It exists within the moment so the individual has access to it at all times under all circumstances. That which is true permeates everything. It permeates trees. It permeates animals. It permeates plants. It permeates humans. It permeates the sky. It permeates the moon. It permeates the stars. It is important for you to understand that that which is true cannot, under any circumstances, be contained within any religion, within any given scientific theorem, within any given personal vendetta, personal power system. It is unlimited, always, therefore, there is no situation in which one individual has a monopoly on the truth. It is in all beings, at all times, in all places.

When Jesus said, " I am the way, the truth, and the life," that which is true is the light, the way within each individual, within each life form unlimited in any way. It was never limited to one individual being. It was always universal. The connection made to that which is true is made in meditation, is made in prayer, is made within the heart. It is not made within dialogue. It is not made within discussion. It is not made within the written word. It is made within the heart. And even within the heart it is unlimited, therefore, there is no monopoly anywhere, at any point, any time. It is an important concept because there is a misconception about the nature of truth at this point which leads to conflict. The conflict that emerges from a belief in truth, like the limited image on the mirror, it does not contain the life that truth itself does, and, therefore, the conflict cannot be resolved on the mirror. It must be resolved within the heart, within meditation, within each individual. The pure in heart see God. It is the pure in heart that are at one with their own being, with their own love, with their own capability, with their own understanding, with their own light within the present time, within the Presence. It is free beyond freedom imagined within this plane of existence.

You will see that the truth is passion in everything. It is simple, a simple love. It is a simple power. It is primarily in the seeking, in the perceiving, in the heart that chooses not stop life as a process. It is inherent within each individual so that when you see an individual whom you truly understand to be very honest, it is an individual who simply seeks within his or her own heart the way without blemish, without selfish motives. The image on the mirror is the image of that individual. What is occurring within that individual is like a prayer. It is like meditation. It is like a constant vigilance. It is hard to understand that all life contains that kind of vigilance. There are plants that seek truth, that seek courage, that seek strength, that, in a sense, pray for strength as they grow as they put all of their energy into the development of the flower. It is all part of the larger metaphysical truth that exists and so is not limited to this plane of existence. Great leaders were individuals who sought with a pure heart the

It is primarily in the seeking, in the perceiving, in the heart that chooses not to stop life as a process. It is inherent within each individual so that when you see an individual whom you truly understand to be very honest, it is an individual who simply seeks within his or her own heart the way without blemish, without selfish motives. The image on the mirror is the image of that individual. What is occurring within that individual is like a prayer. It is like meditation. It is like a constant vigilance

divine direction that was within their own being and would not relinquish the purpose for their life within their own being. They found ways to heal and help by this action of the heart. What becomes reality within your perception of reality exists nowhere but within the initial actions of those who seek the truth within their heart. It is a very personal thing. It is a very private thing. It is very real. Entire nations have sought the same kind truth within the heart of a nation and the resulting experience of others is the joy of the closeness to that which is sought within the heart. The political truth is the most difficult within this realm, but exists within the individual. It is the personal power. It is the personal understanding. It is the personal love. It is the personal prayer that exists.

The Christians believe that the world will be destroyed, but how can you destroy something that is not real. The reality of existence is within the moment, within the Presence, within the present time. You cannot destroy something within the present time.

You will see that the way is clear. It is understood. It is accepted. It is consented to among all life. It is in force. It is occurring. You will see that the truth is in effect as it is in its own nature, the nature of the individual is at one and at peace with the truth. It is at one and at peace with its own being. It is not separated, in any way, from its own nature. It is at one within the Presence—within the presence within the now. The world is transformed. The world is enlightened. It is free of its own limits, its own prejudices, its own fears. You will see that the world is only the image on the mirror. It is only the limited perception of reality. It is not the truth of reality.

It is not the way of reality. It is not real. You cannot destroy something that is not real.

The Christians believe that the world will be destroyed, but how can you destroy something that is not real. The reality of existence is within the moment, within the Presence, within the present time. You cannot destroy something within the present time. The world does not exist. The world does not exist except as anything but the illusion of the world. This is the hardest concept for orthodox Christianity because it has assumed that the world was real and that one came to the world and one was judged by their life here and then one left the world.

And when one left the world, one was destined to the judgment day. That is an illusion. That is a myth. That is a limited concept of what is real. That is not of life. That is not of truth. That is not of love. The illusion is simply the image on the mirror. It is simply an illusion, so when what is what is called an illusion ends, then that is the great trauma that Christians are preparing for when the world does not exist within that illusion, so how could it end. It is not possible. What ends is the illusion. What ends is the perception. What ends is the limited thought. What ends is the belief in fear. What ends is the belief in limits of any kind. And, that is not destructive. It is just vanished. It is gone. It is the same with fog. It simply lifts and what was real remains because it is indestructible, like truth, like the truth that 2+2=4 remains, no matter what is done to it. One could build a city of 2+2=4, and it will remain only as the principle behind the city. The reality is the truth.

It is difficult for individuals to truly understand the nature of reality because they are attached to the image on the mirror. They become attached to these myths, to these concepts of what life is and it is okay for them to be attached to the concepts, but it is fear-based thinking and it is fear-based acting, and it is fear-based understanding, and it is still is not the truth. One could be afraid that 2+2=5 endlessly. It does not alter the truth. It is real. It is the only thing that is real. The being of all life, the love of all life, the truth of all life—all of it is real. There is nothing else.

It is difficult for human life at this point in its history to understand the nature of the ascension because it is imbued with the myth, with the illusion, with the teachings, with the hope of so many at this point.

It is difficult for human life at this point in its history to understand the nature of the ascension because it is imbued with the myth, with the illusion, with the teachings, with the hope of so many at this point. It is disappointing to many that the myth is only that. It is saddening to them. It is difficult for them and, thus, they cling to the story of what they have perceived the world to be. It allows others to cling to the story and, together, they hold on to that which is not true. It is like Copernicus or any other period in human history that individuals have clung to ideas that are illusion and there are so many interpretations of Biblical prophesy that they have created a complex picture form. It is like creating a picture and drawing intricate details to the picture and then looking at the picture assuming that is the truth. The light from which the picture came is the only truth. There is no other truth. The illusion is not the truth. The light is the truth and it is difficult to separate the two. Life itself is all there is. It is unlimited and, therefore, it is difficult for individuals who have made this serious choice to separate themselves from the life they actually live. It is as if the child were in a fog and with no hope of finding its way and the child still existed within the fog. The child exists, period. That is the truth. The fog is the experience, is the limit, is the momentary experience, but it is not the truth. The truth is the child. The truth is the love. The truth is the soul, the spirit of the child. That is the truth. When the fog disappears, the child remains, the love remains, the truth remains.

It is of no consequence, really, that the fog existed and as humanity ascends, it simply releases the illusion. Illusions are more than can be numbered, and one assumes only of human life, but it is also true of all life. When the truth is told, the illusion disappears. It is gone. Where did the illusion go? It never existed.

5

The Nature of Life:

WHAT HAPPENS WITH LIFE, BOTH BEFORE IT COMES HERE AND AFTER IT LEAVES THIS PLANE OF EXISTENCE

Imagine a magnificent field with sunshine and flowers and mountains and sky. The concept of heaven came from the mind of the child. The concept of heaven in the orthodox churches was actually within consciousness long before you arrived here, therefore, it is something that is easy to understand. One assumes that that is what happens when one leaves this plane of existence, but that is what happens, period. There is no hell and no heaven. There is only consciousness. There is only life. The is only the

The concept of heaven in the orthodox churches was actually within consciousness long before you arrived here, therefore, it is something that is easy to understand. One assumes that that is what happens when one leaves this plane of existence, but that is what happens, period. There is no hell and no

energy that permeates all life—the exchange of energy, the existence of energy, the joy of energy, the joy of the energy of love, the joy of the energy of truth, the joy of the energy of existence. You will see that the existence here is one aspect of the whole. It is only a part of part and, therefore, it is easy to understand once you look within.

The scientists have been attempting to understand this plane of existence by looking at the residual, at the past, at the experience here rather than looking within their own being. The enormous shift that is taking place is taking place from "without" to "within." Discoveries are actually made within. Truth is actually found within. Life is actually found within. One assumes that the scientific method is correct because it attempts to objectify the existence without, rather than going to the existence within. That is much like the assumption that the sun revolved around the earth when, in fact, it was not accurate. The same concept is happening that objective reality exists within, not without and scientists will begin to explore the truth of existence. It has taken eons of not finding the truth without to begin to understand what you have called "quantum physics." It is explored within. You will see that growth is part of the existence within. It is not without.

What happens without is that the baby comes to this plane of existence and grows physically, but the growth actually occurs within the individual. One assumes that one is teaching the baby the truth of their existence, for example, by sending them to school and teaching them mathematics and teaching them science and teaching them reading—all the things that are taught in school. But what happens is within the individual, the individual agrees to adapt to the belief systems of this plane of existence. They agree to learn from this plane of existence because they came here to learn from this plane of existence. On another level they function entirely differently at the same time that they function here within this plane of existence. It is like a child can learn four of five or six languages at the same time so that they can learn their own being and retain their own being while still functioning within this plane of existence and growing and expanding and moving into this plane more and more until, eventually, they are caught within the plane of existence and choose to stay.

When you think of dying within this plane of existence, what you are doing is relinquishing your choice to stay. You are not choosing to die. You have become enormously attached to this plane of existence. But, you understand, on another level, that this was only a temporary choice. You exist within other planes, as well, and, therefore, that is how you are capable of loving someone else because that love exists within a separate plane of existence. That is not within this plane of existence, though, ostensibly, it seems to be so. So the attachment with the other being is undistinguished when one leaves this plane of existence. That attachment remains because on another level that attachment exists as part of your own existence. "Other" is part of you. You are part of "other." It is a metaphysical truth.

When Jesus taught that we are not separated from others, he was teaching about the truth of existence. He was not attempting to alter this plane of existence. He was attempting to describe what exits. It is like trying to describe a sunset to a blind person. The blind person can understand, to some degree, what the sunset is, but when one sees the sunset, one automatically understands the nature of the sunset. So it is with the love that exists on this plane of existence, but that has a separate existence as well. It has the solidity of the mountain. It has the solidity of the rock. It is the solid part of your experience. So when Jesus taught, "Do unto others as you would have them do onto you," he was, to some degree, describing the nature of existence. He was less teaching a moral law than telling the truth. There is a difference between the two.

You will see that the way is clear at this point. It is like looking from the top of the mountain at the scenery. It is clear on a clear day. It is easy to see. It is not fogged by fear. It is not fogged by pain. It is not fogged by apprehension. It is clear spiritual understanding of the nature of being. What is being discussed is the nature of all life, all truth, all metaphysical existence. The physical is the offspring of the metaphysical. It is the outcome. It is the product so that what you are seeing is the product of the metaphysical truth. The view from the top of the mountain is one of great distance, great understanding. The view from the top of the mountain in one in which you can see the dynamics of the places below. It is one in which you can understand the greater picture. It is one in which you can understand what exists within the valley, what exists within the sky, what exists within the mountain itself. It is a perspective that humanity is reaching in its great intention to ascend.

The view from the top of the mountain in one in which you can see the dynamics of the places below. It is one in which you can understand the greater picture. It is one in which you can understand what exists within the valley, what exists within the sky, what exists within the mountain itself. It is a perspective that humanity is reaching in its great intention to ascend.

As one ascends, one sees more and more of what existence truly is and what happens is that the linear existence within this plane of existence begins to seem more distant and more distant emotionally—within the heart. The way is so very clear for humanity and the clinging to the valley, the clinging to the specifics, the clinging to the very, very detailed fears is simply giving way.

Life is expanding. Life is ascending. Life is seeking its own nature. Life is reaching for the love that exists within, much as a child reaches for the parent, with open arms. It is joyous. It is loving. It is understanding. It is truthful. The aching of the heart for eons has come to fruition.

You will see that life as you know it is the product of thought, is the product of ideas, is the product of the mind of the individuals creating it. It is not the nature of life itself. The nature of life itself is love itself. The nature of life itself is the light of love. You will see that it is not necessary to generate through the system that has been created. It is not necessary for life to be born, appear, then die. That is the single most revolutionary idea that you face within this plane of existence. You have assumed that life can only emerge through the process of birth, but that is not the case.

You will see that it is not necessary to generate through the system that has been created. It is not necessary for life to be born, appear, then die. That is the single most revolutionary idea that you face within this plane of existence. You have assumed that life can only emerge through the process of birth, but that is not the case.

And, you have assumed that life can only emerge through the use of chemical interaction, and that is not the case. It is important for you to understand that the paradigm that you are dealing with emerges through thought, what can be termed "the Mind of God." It is different from the perception you have of that because what you seek is the Mind of God within your own experience. It is there all of the time within the present. It is not absent. It is always, always there. It is your existence. It is the existence of all life. It is the existence of all truth. It is the existence of all love, but only within the present time. Your life is contingent upon the "light of Love" much like the life of a plant is contingent upon the light that the plant gains. So the question arises, how does life continue? It never does not continue. The reflection on the mirror is the reflection of the experience of individuals, but it is not the nature of the individual, and that is a significant difference that is important for you to understand. The nature of the individual is the substance of the individual. That is why it is recognizable. That is why it appears within the image on the mirror. It is only an image on the mirror. The substance of the individual exists within the light of love. It is their essence. It is their being. It is the truth. It is the soul. It is the spirit. It is the mind. It is all that truly is.

You will see that within this plane of existence, more and more of the appearing of that light of Love is happening. It is becoming recognizable. It is becoming apparent. It is visible. It can be experienced. It can be understood. It can be grasped. The theologians have sought to limit that, but it has exploded beyond any limitations that can be placed upon it so what is occurring with ascension is the presence of the light of Love within each experience. It is permeating each individual's experience. It is overwhelming at times but still can be understood, can be articulated, can be recognized.

You will see that there is much for you to understand as you ascend. There is much for you to appreciate as you ascend. There is much for you to experience as you ascend, but the substance of that ascension exists within the present time, within the individual, within the light of Love and the mind of the Mind of God. It is like the son of the Son…as process.

It is a process in which you simply envision light. You do not need to see the light. You do not need to experience light. You just intend the light and it like opening a window towards it. It allows the individual to see their path even though the words do not come to describe the path. The way becomes more and more clear. That is also done in the process you call prayer or meditation or simple trust—simple love, simple appreciation. All of those elements allow the window of your own being to open and what emerges is the nature of your own being. That is different from the nature of the ego or the self, or the fear, or the pain that is associated with being an individual on this plane of existence. It is the window of what your life truly, is.

Those who have had near-death experiences, have understood this because at that point, they visited their own being. They visited the life of the Life. They visited the love of the Love. They visited the truth of the Truth and then emerged as individuals who understood that larger being.

Many individuals seek their path. They seek to know personally what their path should be when, in fact, it is all encompassing so that when they define their path, they feel comfort that they have described it in words, or "found their way," but what has happened is like a force field has emerged and from that force field, the comfortable level of describing their path is present, however, the activity that actually takes place is the activity of the enormous force field surrounding them which is, in fact, creating the path that they take comfort in within this plane of existence. It is important for you to understand this distinction at this time, because you do not truly understand how this works and in order for you to really understand how this works and how you find your way, you need to understand the nature of your own being, of your own existence, of your own life. It is truly, truly an expression of the larger being. It is not just the individual that appears visually on this plane of existence and, then, at some point, on this plane of existence, dies. It is different from that.

Those who have had near-death experiences, have understood this because at that point, they visited their own being. They visited the life of the Life. They visited the love of the Love. They visited the truth of the Truth and then emerged as individuals who understood that larger being. That larger being is the substance of all life. It is the substance of all truth. It is the background of all mathematics. It is the substance sound of all music. It is the beauty of all art. It is the laughter of a child. It is all things at once and it is acceptable.

The veil, the fog, the pain, the fear of the world of fear—the fear paradigm—the learning by fear is simply lifting. Nothing has changed for the individual. The individual remains the same. The individual functions the same. The individual loves the same, but the veil of fear, the veil of pain is simply being lifted. That is all the ascension ever was. The phrase, "Now we see through a glass, darkly, but then face to Face" is simply what is occurring is simply "the glass, darkly" is no longer.

You will see that there is much to understand at this point. The hope is to understand it because you see the future, but that is not the understanding that you truly seek. The understanding that you seek is within the heart. The heart is the center, the soul, the mind, the truth—all of reality exists, not within the linear sequence of time. It exists within the heart. The shift that is taking place is not within the sequence of time. It is taking place within the heart. It is moving within the heart. It is understood within the heart. The moment at which you meditate, the moment at which you put everything in your mind at rest and move within the heart is the moment at which you enter the place of understanding, the gift of understanding, the reality that exists. The world in the mirror seeks to find the answers on the mirror. It seeks to find the answers outside the reality of existence. It is not possible to find reality outside of existence. It is only possible to find it within the reality of existence so the answers must come from within. They no more can come from the séance, from the vision of the future. It must move within the reality of being.

The shift that is taking place is not within the sequence of time. It is taking place within the heart. It is moving within the heart. It is understood within the heart.

There is difference between that exhibition, that demonstration of being and the understanding of being. The being of each individual is truly all there is and when one moves within, one sees all that is to be seen. One assumes that then it is experience, but it is always experience within and the real change within the earth only exists within the individual. That is all there is.

The difficulty that occurs on the planet is of great consequence. There is great suffering. There is great pain, but the individuals going through those experiences even experience them within their own being. The seeking of the loved one, the seeking of the help for each other, the joy with each other are actually taking place within each individual within the present time. The comfort of that true understanding is immeasurable and diminishes all of the fear and the pain and the agony that is exterior to the individual. When one enters into prayer, one affects the world, one affects reality, one affects the image on the mirror. That is why so very, very many engaged in meditation and prayer at this time in their experience. The engagement that takes place is actually in helping others so that one feels the need to empathetically reach out to others, one needs to move within and use the light and see the individual as free of fear, as free of sorrow, particularly the children and then as the individuals move within and see this, it is actually expressed exterior to the individual and, essentially, move to the image on the mirror. The world is intending to help and the help, therefore, is there, but the true help is within prayer. The true help is with meditation. The true help is within and the greatest revelation of this time is that simple understanding. Place is not as important. Distance is not as important. The experiences exterior to the individual experience, which is the only true reality, show the concept that distance is of little importance, or that place is of little importance which is moving very rapidly to the point at which place is of no importance.

The love, the truth, the beauty, the peace, the life, the joy—all exist within. There is no life but the life within.

You will see that the world is thought. We think, we know, we understand, we feel, we perceive. That is the world. If there is what is called a polar shift or a major shift, it

You will see that the world is thought. We think, we know, we understand, we feel, we perceive. That is the world. If there is what is called a polar shift or a major shift, it is hard for you to understand, at this point, that that is within thought. It is within perception.

is hard for you to understand, at this point, that that is within thought. It is within perception. It is within the individual being so that when the world goes through great changes, it is because it is within. The heart is heavy. The heart is sad. The heart is in pain for others because the individual is not disconnected from others, but it is still contacted within. It is not connected without. Because the eyes see, because there is a visual image, and that is what it is, an image, as discussed earlier, on the mirror. It is light projected on the mirror. It is love projected on the mirror. But the love, the light, the truth are within the individual, so that when one empathizes with another individual's pain, it actually occurs with the individual before it ever appears on the mirror so that the love that is felt appears upon the mirror, but the reality is that it exists within the individual.

The shift in perception is a shift within the world. It is difficult for you to understand that all life is connected to all life. There are no divisions. It is life. It is kingdoms within the mirror, but it is not kingdoms within the individual. Love is light. Love exists. It does not have love that is colored as a mother leopard or a lover. It is light. It is the light of love that exists within each individual life. So that when one goes within, one sees all that is to be seen. The power within the individual is unlimited. It is much, much more far reaching than you have assumed because the theologians have said that you are a limited mortal and a sinner as well. That is the image that is created upon the mirror. That is not the truth of being.

It is very important for you to understand that the shift that is occurring now is the greatest shift of all time. It is the ascension. That which has been taught will diminish to the point where it exists no longer. It is not difficult for you to imagine loving somebody. It is not difficult for you to imagine loving a child or being a child loving a parent. That is easy to imagine. Then you must understand that within the individual the love that exists is unlimited because it is from an unlimited source. That is difficult to imagine, but it is the truth.

SECTION TWO

The world is afraid of earth changes. They are afraid that this is the only plane of existence. They are unwilling to relinquish that belief at this point so they are ill prepared for the time in which humanity ascends and all life ascends. The window into which you are looking through the books is one in which the reality of events is described accurately in terms of their nature. It is a process of sensitizing one to the nature of the larger reality of what is going on. The next section of the book will deal with earth and earth changes from a different perspective. Those who are afraid of earth changes do not understand the nature of reality. They do not understand that this is only one plane of existence. They assume this is all there is and then when they die, this is no longer, that they exist no longer, and that is not the case. So the first chapter of the next section is:

6

EARTH CHANGES

In order to understand earth changes, one must understand the earth. One must understand the nature of the relationship of all life and understand the nature the characteristics of the earth. If one were to describe the earth, one would describe it as a ball of life, a focus of life, a concentration of life, a place of life with myriad forms of life expressing itself. One would not describe it as life-less. One would equate life with the earth. If one were thinking of the universe of ideas, the idea of life would be associated with the earth. Within the realm of the world of fear, is the fear that the only life that exists is the life expressed upon the earth and the scientists spend a great deal of time trying to find life elsewhere. They look to other planets. They do not look within. The greatest shift that is taking place within this paradigm is that they are discovering life within and once that discovery is made then perception of life on the earth will change. The perception of life is that the earth is not the only place that life exists. Life exists on multiple planes of existence within

So as the earth changes, as the earth shifts, as the earth moves, within the realm of thought, it moves into, what is called, the higher planes of existence. It moves within this plane of existence into the higher plane, then life shifts. Life changes. Life evolves quickly. That is called the ascension. Those great leaders who have come before have actually made those shifts physically as well as metaphysically. They understood that life is thought. Life is not physical. It is thought. It is quantum physics. It is unlimited. It is a different realm of existence. It is much, much more than has been described within the scientific world. The scientific world is only coming to the brink of what is already understood within, so that this quantum shift, this ascension is a meld of all thought. It is scientific. It is metaphysical. It is theological. It is "common sense." It is whatever thought categories one subscribes to. It is still thought. The area of exploration to be discovered has taken a quantum leap at this point.

the individual, not exterior to the individual, so the search for life on other planets is not within other planets. The search must begin within. This is simply much more radical than one assumes—that within each individual is the ability of discovering that life in myriad forms, in myriad places, in myriad religions. The use of meditation has helped to connect with other life—prayer, meditation, seeking God has all helped, but the transformation to the ascension occurs within the individual. It is not that the earth is destroyed because the understanding of life that has come into being on the earth cannot be destroyed. Life is indestructible. The image on the mirror is different from the indestructible nature of life itself, so as the earth shifts, as the earth begins to change its own course, as the earth begins to modify its existence, the belief of fear is that it will destroy life. The belief of fear would assume that life only existed here to begin with. The belief of fear is that life is limited to this plane of existence, that is one comes here, lives, and then leaves. The greatest shift is that life is indestructible, that this is just one expression of life itself and that the indestructible concept of life exists within each individual. It is like having, as the expression goes, "your cake and eat it too." You can have the earth and you can have other life as well within your own being simultaneously. Fear based thought would seek fear-based time for the fear based destruction of fear based life. It is not possible. It is an impossibility. One cannot perceive life and be destroyed. It is not even imaginable that that could happen. It is not within the realm of imagination. It cannot happen so the only thing that is destructible is fear based thinking about fear-based life. It does not affect life in any way. The experience of many is beginning to lead

It is like a renaissance. It is like a break-through. It is the moment at which the chicken emerges from the egg and discovers the world beyond the egg. That is what is happening within consciousness at this point. That is the ascension. The chicken remains the chicken, but the perception of the world is beyond what the chicken could have been imagined as the chicken existed in the egg.

into what was presumed to be the destruction of life happened. It did not destroy life. It only enriched it. Life only enriched itself.

You will see that the world is shifting. The planet is actually shifting. It is moving in ways that have not yet been detected. It is changing its course. That is not a fearful thing. That is not to be feared. Those who will seek fear will not be satisfied with the shift because it is not a fearful shift. The earth has always changed its course. The earth has always moved. It is nothing new. The life that you express on this plane of existence is also changing. It has always changed, will always change because it is the nature of life to change. It is not anything new to life to constantly change its form. Those who teach evolution understand that because evolution means that life is always changing its form, so that is not a fearful thing. Life has always been adaptable to whatever form it may take. It is difficult to imagine that life itself is much more massive than you can understand, but should you understand that this is but one plane of existence and that life takes place on many planes of existence within, then you understand that the life that is expressed here is only a segment of a segment of a segment. It is not the whole. The whole is beyond imagination. The whole has been termed God. The whole has been termed unlimited joy, but the limits that have been placed upon it are only limits of thought. They are limits of experience. They are limits of paradigm. The life itself is, truly, unlimited.

So as the earth changes, as the earth shifts, as the earth moves, within the realm of thought, it moves into, what is called, the higher planes of existence. It moves within this plane of existence into the higher plane, then life shifts. Life changes. Life evolves quickly. That is called the ascension. Those great leaders who have come before have actually made those shifts physically as well as metaphysically. They understood that life is thought. Life is not physical. It is thought. It is quantum physics. It is unlimited. It is a different realm of existence. It is much, much more than has been described within the scientific world. The scientific world is only coming to the brink of what is already understood within, so that this quantum shift, this ascension is a meld of all thought. It is scientific. It is metaphysical. It is theological. It is "common sense." It is whatever thought categories one subscribes to. It is still thought. The area of exploration to be discovered has taken a quantum leap at this point. It is like a renaissance. It is like a break-through. It is the moment at which the chicken emerges from the egg and discovers the world beyond the egg. That is what is happening within consciousness at this point. That is the ascension. The chicken remains the chicken, but the perception of the world is beyond what the chicken could have been imagined as the chicken existed in the egg.

You will see that those who seek fear will relinquish that fear in ways you cannot foresee. It is not by the Christian doctrine of repentance. It is through other means within the individual. The individual is all there is and when the fear of earth changes and retribution and anger and lack and all of the fear-based thinking actually comes to a head. then the change is immediate. It is like any other festering situation. Once the pressure is relieved, all of the accumulated substance is gone—it

The fear of lack, the fear of pain, the fear of sadness, the fear of sin, the fear of sorrow, the fear of all of the elements of what is called the world of fear are only like the mist in the garden and when the fog lifts, the fog is gone. When the fear lifts, it is gone. It does not have anything to do with earth changes anymore.

is no longer. It is gone. The fear of lack, the fear of pain, the fear of sadness, the fear of sin, the fear of sorrow, the fear of all of the elements of what is called the world of fear are only like the mist in the garden and when the fog lifts, the fog is gone. When the fear lifts, it is gone. It does not have anything to do with earth changes anymore.

The individuals who seek fear are gone, but not spiritually. It is like the image is gone, like the pain is gone, like the result is gone. You will see that there is much to understand in a fairly short time. There is much to understand about the nature of love, the nature of the truth, the nature of life itself. It is like quantum physics. It is a breakthrough. The books are a breakthrough as well to understand the nature of life, to understand where explorations must occur at this point in order to truly understand the events that are taking place around the individuals on this plane of existence. It is a huge, quantum leap. It is beyond imagination. The physicists do not understand it. The scientists do not understand it. The theologians do not understand it because they have relinquished their understanding of the power of unlimited love. It is like a paradigm shift. It is, as the analogy that was given, when the chick comes out of the egg into the whole world, at that point, the shift occurs.

The world still does not understand that there is no fear involved in this shift. There is no pain. There is no sorrow. There is no turbulence. There are no physical changes. It occurs within life. All of it occurs within life. It does not occur within the image projected on the mirror. It occurs within the second. It occurs within the present. It occurs within life itself. That is the greatest shift of all because the shift that occurs within life itself is beyond the earth. It is beyond the universe as you know it. It is perception and perception is beyond the earth. It is beyond the universe. It is the Mind of God. It is within the Mind of God.

It is like a bird that is suddenly taken up. It is not the rapture described by the Christians. It is beyond that perception. It is not that a few are taken up. It is that life shifts within itself. The Christ consciousness that is described by the Christians is, essentially, life that makes that shift within itself. It is not dissimilar to those who have been through a near-death experience. It is not death, but life. And the theologians have missed the point. They have not understood that when one dies, one simply returns to the nature of their own being within the present time. It is important, at this point, that the world understands this difference. It is essential.

The books are here in order so that can happen.

It is within. It is not without. It is within. It is not a movement. It is not a religion. It is not a scientific discovery. It is the nature of being within the individual, within the connectivity to life, within the power of life, within the love of life, within the present understanding of life. It all exists within the individual. It exists within the present. It exists now, so that when the ascension occurs, it occurs within the now. It occurs within the individual now, not in the future when some fearful event takes place, but within the present, within the now and the individual is at peace with that, within the now. The individual is loving that within the now. The individual is free within the now.

There is nothing that cannot be feared in some form or another. Imagine seeing a situation in which there was, simply, no room for fear. There was no room for pain, for sorrow or unkindness or cruelty in any form.

You will see that the world is afraid of its own being. It's afraid of its nature. It's afraid of its character. It's afraid of its beauty. Within the world of fear, there is everything to fear. One could fear love. One could fear God. One could fear life. One could fear death. One could fear war. One could fear sorrow. One could fear everything. There is nothing that cannot be feared in some form or another. Imagine seeing a situation in which there was, simply, no room for fear. There was no room for pain, for sorrow or unkindness or cruelty in any form.

It is difficult to extract from what exists as a fear-based thought, the substance that has never changed within the earth. The reality of the earth and the reality of life is the nature of love, is the nature of truth, is the nature of spirit that exists. That is all that exists, truly, so that the fear-based thought, like the fog that vanishes, simply vanishes. Does that alter the earth? Does that alter life? Does that alter anything? No, it does not. It only vanishes and what remains is what always existed, what has always been the nature of being.

The heart has longed for this for a very long time. The heart is like the center of the individual within the present time. It is where life occurs, so when one discovers what life is all about, one goes within the heart. One goes within the place of all of the human activities that exist. Within that specific place, it is important that you understand that the way is ready. The way is prepared within the heart. The way is cleared. The way is enlarged within the heart. It is the place of the heart. It is the present of the heart. It is the presence of the individual within the heart, within the soul, within the mind, within the spirit that occurs within any given second.

You will see that the world is ready for its understanding of what is occurring within the individual. It is ready to see visually what has already occurred. The ascension has already occurred. The ascension is occurring within. It is occurring within each life form, within each life kingdom, within each life manifest within the earth itself. The fear is that the earth will shift and that life will be destroyed and that is why the books are here so that you will understand that the earth is not being destroyed. The earth is not being torn asunder. It is not being thrown somewhere into space. It is simply shifting. It is not destructive. It is enhancing. It is ascending. It is difficult to understand because you assume this plane of existence is all there is. You assume that the form the earth takes is the only possible form for the earth, but attempt to imagine the earth in harmony with itself. Imagine that life is in harmony with itself, at peace with itself and within its own nature filled with love and filled with joy. It is difficult to imagine.

It is difficult to extract from what exists as a fear-based thought, the substance that has never changed within the earth. The reality of the earth and the reality of life is the nature of love, is the nature of truth, is the nature of spirit that exists. That is all that exists, truly, so that the fear-based thought, like the fog that vanishes, simply vanishes. Does that alter the earth? Does that alter life? Does that alter anything? No, it does not. It only vanishes and what remains is what always existed, what has always been the nature of being. Those who have died and returned know that that is the nature of being. They know that that is all there is. They have emerged from the fear-based thought within themselves because they understand the nature of life because they were at one and at peace with it.

So, the religions that created the image on the mirror, that created the paradigm, that you encounter, that you call life on earth, will no longer control the lives of those who express that life, that being, that God—the Mind of God. The religions simply attempted to control and create a paradigm. The paradigm leaves. The paradigm no longer exists. Does religion exist then? Not in its present form. It does not exist. For it truly only existed within each individual. It is within the present time. The most difficult concept for you to understand is the nature of the present time. It simply the only reality is the present time. That is all there is. There is nothing else. And so the image on the mirror—the strife, the pain, the sorrow, do not exist within the present. They do *NOT* exist within the present time. So, nothing truly has changed except the image, *THE IMAGE*, on the mirror, the image that has been created within the mind of not just man, but of life.

The ascension is the most natural process there is there is because it is the nature of the nature of life.

So you will see that what the religions have termed Armageddon, or the end of the world, or the rapture or the second coming is all within the individual.

So you will see that what the religions have termed Armageddon, or the end of the world, or the rapture or the second coming is all within the individual. It is not within social groups. It is not within a huge shift in the physical earth, or the coming down of the stars, or anything as dramatic as that would portend. It is in the individual. The joy of the second coming is within the individual. The joy of the rapture, the joy of the shift of the ascension is within the individual. It is not exterior to any life. It is within the life. It is certainly less dramatic, but it is true. It is what the Masters understood from the life they experienced—that it all is within. Nothing is exterior to the individual, that all life exists within, that exploration of space, that exploration of time, that exploration of quantum physics, everything exists within life itself. The shift in paradigm, the earth changes, the shift within is the understanding that it exists within, that the earth exists within life, that life does not exist within the earth, that all life exists within and that existence is unlimited. That existence is truly, by nature, that of the Mind of God. There is no fear. There is no pain. There is no sorrow. All things pass away. The scales fall from before the eyes and the existence that has always been there, remains. This is a very important concept to understand as one begins to understand the events that are taking place at this point within each individual life.

The image on the mirror is shifting because the life is shifting.

You will see that as the earth begins to free itself in the world of thought from fear based thinking, it returns to its natural harmony. It returns a state itself of peace. It is not like the

The Elysian Fields, the idea of heaven, the concept of Valhalla or any other concept that has come in consciousness is simply the life that expresses within the present time. It is like that life is sought within the image on the mirror, but the image on the mirror is incapable of replicating that life exactly. It is incapable of the dynamism that occurs within the present time. It is incapable of the love, the peace, the joy, the spirit, the soul, the mind that is existent within the present time.

peace you seek among peoples in which you find no animosity. It is like a peace that truly "passes all understanding." It is like a peace that is not understood yet. It is a peace within. It is a peace that involved all life at peace with itself. The Elysian Fields, the idea of heaven, the concept of Valhalla or any other concept that has come in consciousness is simply the life that expresses within the present time. It is like that life is sought within the image on the mirror, but the image on the mirror is incapable of replicating that life exactly. It is incapable of the dynamism that occurs within the present time. It is incapable of the love, the peace, the joy, the spirit, the soul, the mind that is existent within the present time.

So, the earth itself which is life, which is a collection of all life within this plane of existence is a peace, is at one, it is in harmony. You will use the light and see that peace as you meditate. It exists. The individuals who have been led to do the books, to meditate, to seek this ascension are all encompassing. All life has sought this plane of existence, this peace within itself. You will see that when you leave the world of fear, when you leave this fear-based thought, as you are at this point, you do not see a smooth transition. You see a rugged one. You see one that seems to have difficulty in it, but there is point at which it ceases to be difficult. It ceases to be rugged. It ceases to be less than harmonious, and that is within. You will now cease to find your peace in the image on the mirror. You will find in within all life. You will find it within at this point. The world has collectively chosen to relinquish the idea of, for example, nuclear war or conquering others. It is moving quickly away from all of those concepts that have been so very destructive within consciousness. The concept of nuclear war came from the belief that one had to protect oneself at all costs, but the use communication across the earth has allowed individuals to understand that there is no protection. There is no balance of terror. There is no way that life does not interact with other life. The idea of protecting oneself is simply not necessary at this point because there is a larger understanding that that is not possible—the idea of sharing the earth, the idea of sharing the resources of the earth. The idea of sharing life with each other is becoming more and more prevalent to the point where it ceases to be important to be defensive. It ceases to be important to be protective of each other. These are ideals that have been sought for many, many generations. It is actually reaching a point where it is acceptable at this point of existence. It is symptomatic of the transition that is going on during the ascension, the change of consciousness within each individual. It is very subtle. Those who pray must continue to pray. They must continue to use the light. They must continue to meditate. The concepts that have evolved in the world of fear lose their charm. They lose their attraction. They lose their ability to attract others to the concepts themselves. This too is part of the enormous transition in thought that is occurring. You will see that the world is preparing itself for its own ascension within. It is difficult to imagine the earth itself as living, but it is living.

7

Life within Life

You will see that when a flower blossoms, it takes tremendous energy for the flower to blossom. All of the energy of the flower goes into the blossom. It works very hard to create the beauty of the blossom, the color of the blossom, the life of the blossom. So it is with life at this point. It is taking all of its energy to create the ascension, to create the blossom, to create the transition. As a result there are many, many individuals who are in meditation a great deal at this point. They are making abrupt changes in their lives. They are exploring things they have never explored before. They are feeling compelled to meditate, to pray, to even join churches, or to become part of religious movements and all of that is part of the effort of the life here to blossom, to create the ascension for itself.

It seems like that becomes a conflict with other life, but it really isn't. It is within the individual and therefore the Muslims are much more devoted as Muslims and the Christians are much more devoted as Christians and those who meditate, meditate more frequently, and those who seek God within, seek it more earnestly. That is all an effort to create the blossom of the ascension.

There are some who are afraid of this blossoming, but, on the whole, life itself is at a peak of its energy, as it puts forth all of its energy in order to create the blossom that is the ascension. It is an important time. It is an important effort.

You will see that when a flower blossoms, it takes tremendous energy for the flower to blossom. All of the energy of the flower goes into the blossom. It works very hard to create the beauty of the blossom, the color of the blossom, the life of the blossom. So it is with life at this point. It is taking all of its energy to create the ascension, to create the blossom, to create the transition.

For the flower to blossom, it is essential to the flower. It cannot say to itself, "I will not blossom. I will not produce the blossom when the time is right." It cannot help itself. It simply moves into the kind of energy it takes to create the blossom, and beyond. But, it is of great importance for the survival of the flower that the flower simply do as it is meant to do.

It is difficult for you to even imagine the kind of effort that is taking place at this point within the present time, within the meditation, within the moment before you realize that you have been hit by a wave. It is that moment within the present time that all of this effort is taking place. It is not taking place in the image on the mirror. It is taking place within and it is the greatest of all moments within history. It is the apex. It is the glorious coming of the ascension.

It does not seem that way to so many, but it is happening. It is like each individual is compelled in their own way, in their unique way to participate in this enormous change. You do not understand that all life is doing this, but it is. The life is within life. The life that is engaged in this effort is life within life. It is the life that exists in the moment, in the present. It is like the cells of plant. It is like the cells of the individual. It is like the life within the form that is life. You will see that each individual has a purpose and it will be much easier now to articulate the purpose of each individual in this process. It is almost as if part of the plant is the yellow in front or the green in the back. Each different part of the plant actually creates the entire blossom. It is not that every cell of the plant knows its whole role in the creation of the flower, but, in fact, that is how it is working for individuals on this plane of existence. Each individual is contributing as they must in order for the entire picture to become a blossom, to become what it must become, so one individual may feel the compulsion to meditate and another individual may feel the compulsion to pray, and another individual may feel the compulsion to seek psychically to help others, and there is an infinite variety of the possibilities of what each individual's role will be and is at this point, but it is occurring and the purpose does not necessarily have to be articulated. It only exists within the individual so they will not be able not to do what they must do in the flowering of the plant. It is like the cells that become the flower cannot help but becoming the cells that create flower. That is what is happening within this plane of existence at this point.

There is fear that that is not the case, but it is the case. It is within the Mind of God. It is a divine plan. It is a Divine purpose for humanity, for all life here on this plane of existence. The scope of this is beyond what you can imagine, but it still can be understood. It can be appreciated. It can be accepted without fear.

You will see the connectivity of all life more and more clearly. You will begin to see the ebb and the flow of the consciousness of each individual connecting with each other individual so that as the individuals create the flower or begin to create, together, the ascension, the relationship becomes more and more connected. It becomes more and more a part of the whole. It is not without design that the internet exists and that this connectivity takes place in myriad forms at this point. It is part of the nature of being. The life as it emerges is of great beauty and begins to be more and more recognizable among those who are seeing it clearly. The way is becoming clearer for all life and all kingdoms and phylum of each species and is contributing its own unique energy to the creation of the entire picture.

You will see the connectivity of all life more and more clearly. You will begin to see the ebb and the flow of the consciousness of each individual connecting with each other individual so that as the individuals create the flower or begin to create, together, the ascension, the relationship becomes more and more connected. It becomes more and more a part of the whole.

It is like when humans began to look upon the earth from space, they saw a ball of life. It was glowing. It was beautiful. It was life. It was one. It was unique. It was alive. The way is becoming available for all to enjoy the process, rather than struggle through the process. It is much easier to flow downstream rather than to fight the current and, in a sense, life is beginning to flow downstream with other life rather than fighting the current. Those who seem dissident, those who are very angry or those who feel the need to impose a given thought upon another being are beginning to give way to the current of allowing each life to have its own expression—both physically and metaphysically. You will not be afraid of the period ahead when you truly begin to see the nature of the development as it occurs. The river of life is truly a river of life. It is a joyous process within that river.

8

The Nature of the Singular Moment

THE PRESENT MOMENT

The book has discussed the present time. That is different from a present moment. Those are distinctly different ideas. The present time is the continuum in which the individual exists, is present, is a presence, is part of the Presence. It is all the same thing. It is a continuum. It is not the moment in the present time. There is a difference.

The moment is an experience within the continuum and exists as a separate entity. It is a movement within the moment. The movement is the thought that exists. It is the nature of thought. So that thoughts exists as moments within the continuum of the present time.

Thoughts are much more than you assume. A thought is an energy, a unique experience. It is without category. It is without limits. If one had a thought, it could exist at any place, at any point. It does not have a limit. It does not have a point at which it exists and then ceases to exist. It always exists, once it is experienced. The body of thoughts is unlimited. It is without measure. That is the abundance that

Thoughts are much more than you assume. A thought is an energy, a unique experience. It is without category. It is without limits. If one had a thought, it could exist at any place, at any point. It does not have a limit. It does not have a point at which it exists and then ceases to exist. It always exists, once it is experienced. The body of thoughts is unlimited. It is without measure. That is the abundance that exists for the individual.

exists for the individual. It is without I.Q. It is without limitation in expression. It has unlimited expression within the continuum of the present time, but emerges on the mirror and the image on the mirror is the aftermath of the unlimited nature of thought. The image on the mirror assumes a limit. It assumes a finite limit to the number of thoughts that can be expressed which is not the nature of the individual, which is not the nature of the moment within the present time, so when it comes, for example, to problem solving, the image on the mirror is only a miniscule part of the process of problem solving for the individual. It is infinitesimal piece of the puzzle that has actually occurred that solves a problem. That is why problems can be solved in myriad ways because the possibilities and the permutations and combinations are endless. It is like fear-based thought chooses to limit thought out of fear because one wants to be secure in what one encounters so that one will not be afraid, but the irony is that one limiting the possible solutions to the problem and, therefore, creating a more fearful situation for the individual. Fear-based thinking is limited perception of unlimited thought. When it comes to solving the problems that individuals encounter, the solutions, again, are found within meditation more than it does without meditation, therefore, when one says one will pray on the matter or one will meditate on the matter, one is actually tapping into an unlimited possibility of solutions to the problem. That will be important in the time ahead—to use the tool available through problem solving.

You will see that the moment is truly what exists within the continuum of the present time. That is the building block for everything that happens. It is the creative tool from which the world has begun. The image on the mirror is created by the moment within the continuum of the present time. It is important for the whole realm of physics to begin to understand what is termed the moment. It is important for them to explore within life itself.

You will see that the moment is truly what exists within the continuum of the present time. That is the building block for everything that happens. It is the creative tool from which the world has begun. The image on the mirror is created by the moment within the continuum of the present time. It is important for the whole realm of physics to begin to understand what is termed the moment. It is important for them to explore within life itself.

It is the next step in the area of physics. It is beyond quantum physics. The books deal with the nature of reality. They do not deal with theology. They deal with what is real and they are important because they lead the way for the realm of physics to begin to understand itself, to understand the physical universe, to understand the nature of what exists. What exists is the individual being within the present time, within the moment. The world that you experience emerges from that reality. So that when you begin to truly explore the nature of the present time and what is termed, the moment, then you will begin to understand the nature of physics, the nature of science, of mathematics, of music, of anything that you seek within the image upon the mirror. It exists within. It does not exist without and to explore it on the mirror as has been said is to not understand its nature. It is like a child who assumed that he or she did not need to understand mathematics in order to understand mathematics. But to simply play with numbers without understanding the principles behind mathematics. As the child understands what mathematics is, how it functions, they are able to work it within their own lives. They are able to add groceries. They are able add money. They are able to add whatever er they have to have, but they must first understand it from within themselves. What happen outside of themselves is only an expression of what happens within—the motive within, the spirit within, the love within, the life within, the truth within.

You are truly moving beyond the need for death. Death is only a creation. It is only part of a belief system. What exists does not die and one does not need the vehicle of death in order to connect with what exists. It is truly a belief. It is truly a projection upon the mirror. It does not relate to the nature of reality.

So, if one can imagine the moment, one can imagine. For example, imagine a moment when you loved someone with all of your heart. What existed was within the present time. The moment at which you love exists within the present time. It does not exist within the poetry that is written about love or the expression to others about that love. What exists within is where love actually occurs. So to assume that love exists within the image on the mirror, is not accurate.

Love exists within the heart, within the present, within the Presence and ultimately within the Mind of God. It exists. It does not exist separate from the moment. It exists within the moment. It exists forever within the moment, within the present. It is not dependent upon a physical thing. It is not dependent upon a place, an object, or an element. It is dependent upon what exists within the moment, within the present, within the Presence. It is difficult for you to imagine that the only reality is the present time, the moment, but that is all that exists. There is nothing else.

You will see that the moment is the place in which you develop the ideas that create the reality on this plane of existence. It is the source of experience. It is the source of the paradigm that you encounter, but it is essentially coming though the fog of the fear-based thinking so that the experience here is encased within the fog of fear-based thinking. It is becoming very, very apparent to individuals on this plane of existence that the fog is, in fact, lifting. It is simply disappearing into the mist. As this occurs then the creation of the moment, the creation of the present time, the creation of unlimited love has its clear reflection on the mirror. It is not obstructed and filtered through the filter of the fear-based thinking, of the limited thought. It has been a great burden for humanity and all life to encounter fear-based thinking because by nature, it is love.

You will see that the moment is the place in which you develop the ideas that create the reality on this plane of existence. It is the source of experience.

It is like there is a dichotomy within this plane of existence because of that fact—that fog, that limit. It is a burden that is carried here by those who come, but is no longer necessary. It is easy to exist free of the fog of fear-based thinking. It is easy to exist outside of the fog of fear-based theology. It is easy to exist outside of the fog of fear-based governmental systems, of social systems, of relationships, of fear-based anything, fear-based relationships with children, fear-based relationships with plants. It is easy to exist outside of that realm and a great comfort to those who actually begin to experience that. It is of the heart. It is of the clarity of the heart. It is of the freedom of the heart. It is the heart, which is the reality of the individual free to be what the individual truly is.

When the mist vanishes, the mist is gone. It vanishes. It is no longer. That is the ascension. That is the freedom that is being achieved within thought, within the moment, within the present, within the Presence.

9

LOVE AS POWER

THE ONLY POWER, ULTIMATELY

You will see that the love that is experienced in the present time is overwhelming the world of fear. It is in abundance. It is unlimited. It is permeating everything. It has power beyond your greatest imagination because it lives within the individual. It is the nature of the individual. It is the nature of all life. It is characteristic of all life. All life loves—all life. So as the fog begins to lift, the love pours in quantities you cannot imagine. "There is no fear in love for perfect love casts out fear." It is a fact. It is not a theory. It is the truth of being that love has no limit. It has no death. It has no going or

So when one is looking at the ascension, one understands that what is happening in the ascension is the creation of the normalization of life itself. It is simply coming into its own being. And what appears on the mirror is a reflection of that coming into its own.

coming. It is the stable par of reality. It is reality itself and that love is unstoppable. It is unlimited. It is the impetus behind even the actions of the image on the mirror. It is the impetus behind the creation of the generations. It is the impetus behind the creation of a nation. It is the impetus behind the offspring of all life. It is like looking at a field and understanding that everything in the field has been created by love—the offspring, the flowers, the sunset, the rocks, the air. It is the creation of love itself. So when one is looking at the ascension, one understands that what is happening in the ascension is the creation of the normalization of life itself. It is simply coming into its own being. And what appears on the mirror is a reflection of that coming into its own.

This is the dark before the dawn, but the dawn is there and all life understands that at this point. Each individual brings it into being in their own way. It is difficult to understand how this happens at this point, but it is, in fact, happening. That is why the books must come out at this point. You will see that love is all. That is the reality of being. That is not a theory. That is not a hope. That is a fact.

They assumed that it might come in a white robed man who came to save humanity or whatever theological belief is subscribed to, but that is not the case. It occurs within the heart. It occurs within empathy for all life. It occurs within the power of love itself, within the moment within the present time, within the Presence.

It is important for you to understand that the power of love is the only power, ultimately. It is difficult to see within the largest of all pictures, which is to see from the presence within the Presence. It is love that motivates the individual. It is love that motivates the world. It is love that motivates, ultimately, the stars. It is the power behind the power. It is not the pseudo-love. It is not even the image upon the mirror. It is the love within. It is the power within. It is the life within. It is what those who have been through the near-death experience, experienced. That is the power that exists. It is power beyond any human power, any planetary power. It is, ultimately, the only power. There are those who fear love, who are afraid of its effect on the world, but that is only fear-based thinking. That is only attempting to limit that which is limitless. It exists within the heart. It exists within the deepest parts of the individual and as it occurs, within the moment, within the present time continuum, it is undeniable to the individual.

And, it is undeniable to all life. One assumes that plants and animals do not experience deep and profound love, but they truly do. It is difficult for you to understand that plants experience great love for those who care for them and those who nurture them and those who pay attention to them and to their offspring. There are all of the elements that humans have within the realm of the plant. There is pride in the flower. There is joy in growth. There is the joy of being warmed by the sun. It is all part of the experience of the plant kingdom of life as well as the animal kingdom of life. It is all part of the life continuum—the connectivity of all life. Then when the ascension occurs, it does not just occur for humans, as we have said many times. It occurs for plants and animals and all life. It is the understanding that occurs within each form of life from the perspective of the kingdom of that life. And that is all that is, like the perspective of those who prescribe to different theological beliefs. It is a kingdom within a kingdom and is acceptable. It is clear love. It is clear power.

You will see that as the ascension occurs, the individuals are free of the constraints upon that love. Fear-based thought would mean it would not be a positive effect, but, in fact, it is the most positive effect of all because contained within the love is the empathy for those around, the connectivity with those around and true love means the connectivity of all life. So that when love occurs it isn't that there is undue sexual behavior or anything else, it means that there is such empathy with all life, the heart grows. The heart swells. The heart enlarges as the largess of the heart becomes so great that the joy for the individual becomes overwhelming. It is what the ages have longed for. They assumed that it might come in a white robed man who came to save humanity or whatever theological belief is subscribed to, but that is not the case. It occurs within the heart. It occurs within empathy for all life. It occurs within the power of love itself, within the moment within the present time, within the Presence.

So the period ahead is one in which the limits of the fear of love are to come to a head, to come to a point in which it is unnecessary to deal with problems in a way in which it is harmful to others. That is the Biblical prophesy of the end of war. But, truly, it is the end of war. It is the end of using armaments and pain and death to achieve a given goal. It is not necessary. It is fear—fear of lack, fear of powerlessness, fear of the unknown in terms of the sincere love of others for various religions, various

Humanity has reached a point in which it will no longer tolerate war. It will no longer tolerate problem solving in terms of war. It is at a very critical point and it is very important this year that those who are given the need to pray and meditate, do so. It is very important.

cultural systems. Humanity has reached a point in which it will no longer tolerate war. It will no longer tolerate problem solving in terms of war. It is at a very critical point and it is very important this year that those who are given the need to pray and meditate, do so. It is very important. The world is ready to relinquish war. It is ready to isolate those who seek it and limit their role in the world. It is ready to systematically relinquish all idea of war. You do not understand, but it has come from the larger being. It is like the prayer that is done before the way opens up in a given situation. The prayer cycle has been completed. The way is clear. It is not a hope. It is a fact of physics, of the nature of being, of the truth.

10

The Search for Reality

THE SEARCH FOR THAT WHICH IS REAL

You will see that the use of meditation is the search for that which is true, for that which is the underlying power, that which is, like the mountains, solid, permanent and unchanging. It is the essential creativity that comes with creating the image on the mirror. The image on the mirror is created through that which is real, that which is permanent, that which is solid, that which is truth, that which is love, that which is unlimited, the mind of God, unlimited in its capabilities. It is difficult for you to imagine that the only reality is love. There is no other reality.

You will see that the use of meditation is the search for that which is true, for that which is the underlying power, that which is, like the mountains, solid, permanent and unchanging.

You assume that when you love someone here on this plane of existence that that is the nature of love itself, and it is, but it is an expression of that love, it is not the nature of that love. It is within the individual, so the feeling of love generates from the individual and is always present. It is always there even when relationships fall apart or dissolve, there is an element of that love which is there. It stays. It stays essentially within the heart because that is what is real. That is what is true. So if the relationship dissolves, the truth of the relationship, which is love, does not entirely dissolve. It does not entirely change because it is changeless.

It is the moment within the present time. It is that which never disappears. It cannot disappear because the individual remains. So that which real is the metaphysical truth. That which is changeable which is evolving is the image on the mirror. The substance is what is occurring within. It is occurring with power beyond you greatest imagination.

So that every individual within this plane of existence contains within themselves that power, that window to the universe and beyond. Every individual contains within themselves the mind of God—the unlimited potential, the unlimited joy, the unlimited love. It is beyond reverence for life, it is understanding power.

You can actually see it in the eyes of individuals. You can see the power, the light, the joy, the existence of the infinite within. It is not that, eventually, you have eternal life. It is that you are within eternal life—unlimited life. You are the life of life itself, so when to truly understanding the nature of that which is real, one needs only to look in the eyes of others, to the nature of their nature. One then understands the nature of the ascension, because one sees the power that exists. One understands the power of the ascension because one sees within the individual the power that exists. One understands the power of the ascension because one understands what exists in the power of the individual. Simply look into their eyes. You will see it.

It is the next greatest area of exploration, to truly see what exists within. So when one experiences physical disasters and it looks as though the individual has left this plane of existence, it is very important to understand that they never existed within this plane of existence. What existed was what you saw when you saw their individuality, when you saw the nature of their nature, when you saw the love of their love, when you felt their presence within your own heart. That is the moment in which you understood that this is not real. This is unreal but reflects the real. It is the image on the mirror that verifies what exists, what is real, what is real now within the present within this room, within this day. Nothing is destroyed within this room, within the present, within this day. It exists.

You will see that the world is beginning to truly understand that reality. It is beginning to move beyond the fear, the pain, the disasters, the theoretical earth changes, the tsunamis, the elements, the permutation and combinations of the creation of reality on the mirror. It is moving beyond that and beginning to look within the heart within the present time, within the presence within the Presence. The more one meditate, the more one moves to that place within the heart, within the present. It is a tremendous movement for humanity and is occurring globally. It is a shift in consciousness.

One intuitively knows that when one loves another, there is an element of that love that never dies. It simply doesn't. There are times when one wishes that it would, but it does not. So, the reality is within the present time within the Presence, the image on the mirror is the expression of that reality.

So, continuing that which is real. That which is real is unchanging within its core, within its substance. The nature of love is not quantifiable. You cannot measure x number of megawatts of love. It goes back to its own source, which is unlimited. You can, within the image on the mirror, assume that one can love for a limited period of time but there is an intuitive knowledge that love exists far beyond that period of time and the world has a difficult time articulating the nature of love itself. It seldom tries because it is confused. It is confusing. It is confusing to observe the relationship within the image on the mirror and understand there is an element that goes back to something that the individual is not sure of within the present time, but it has not been clearly understood until the exploration within the individual begins, then it is to be explored and understood and appreciated. One intuitively know that when one loves another, there is an element of that love that never dies. It simply doesn't. There are times when one wishes that it would, but it does not. So, the reality is within the present time within the Presence, the image on the mirror is the expression of that reality. There is a disorientation in terms of how it actually works. It actually works within the present time, within the Presence. It does not work that one loves for an eternity. That is not how that works. That love exists within the present time within the Presence and there is no eternity projected on the image on the mirror. That simply is a myth, a hypothesis that has no basis in fact. The power of that love is only now beginning to be understood, because the power of that love exists within the heart. It cannot exist within the intellectual community. It cannot exist within an analysis of an analysis. It has to exist within the heart. It flows and ebbs within the heart. So the image on the mirror cannot define love. It cannot utilize the love that exists. It abuses it. It misuses it. The only place in which in an infinitesimal way is within the clarity of the heart, the motive of the heart, the purity of the heart. It is like the heart becomes like a beautiful, clear glass through which that love shines into the image on the mirror. And that power is beginning to be tapped into, barely. As humanity continues to pray and create the ascension through global prayer and meditation as was discussed in the section dealing with the creation of flower by the plant—as humanity begins to create the ascension through this great surge of prayer and meditation, then the power of love begins to come clearly through and transform the image on the mirror. It really is not complicated, but the orientation has been corrected. Part of the book is to create a correct alignment of ideas.

You will see that the world is ready to understand the image on the mirror and what is real. It is willing to begin to explore the reality of the nature of the individual and begin to cease turning its head from the exploration of love, of the heart, of the power of love. It has been stated by many spiritual leaders. It has been advocated that humanity explore the power of love. It has been advocated that the power of love be tapped into, but humanity has had a difficult time in that area of exploration. It has explored what it calls the physical universe, and physics, and chemistry, and mathematics and all areas but the power of love. It has sought nuclear energy and any form of energy it could find,

It has explored what it calls the physical universe, and physics, and chemistry, and mathematics and all areas but the power of love. It has sought nuclear energy and any form of energy it could find, but ignored the greatest and only power that exists.

but ignored the greatest and only power that exists. That is the power of love. It has not sought with the use of its scientists and any of the major disciplines to truly explore this area within the individual. It can no longer be ignored. It can no longer be not sought as the only means to power—any kind of power—any kind.

The image on the mirror is the expression of part of what exists within the individual, but the power that exists within the individual is within the heart. It is the next area of major exploration. It is beyond quantum physics. It is the areas that must and will be explored. It has essentially already happens as the ascension occurs. The individuals understand this. They have, essentially, created the flower. They have created the ascension. It is coming into blossom. It is being supported at all levels in all places, in all nations, among all life globally. So it will be a simple process in many ways. It is like flowing downstream. It simply will occur.

So, in this area of reality you will understand that reality is simply is that which truly exists within the present time within the Presence.

SECTION THREE

11

The Dream and the Dreamer

THE NATURE OF THE PRESENT WITHIN THE DREAM

You will see that as you ascend within the framework of unlimited love, it is, to some degree like dreaming. It is like the shift in consciousness becomes more real that what has been termed "real" so that the dream becomes reality and reality becomes the dream. The reality of taxes or whatever linear, sequential thought process has seemed so very important becomes less and less important and what becomes important is the exciting discovery process within the consciousness of the individual. It is the realization of the dreams. It is much like when one sets a goal and then dream

You will see that as you ascend within the framework of unlimited love, it is, to some degree like dreaming. It is like the shift in consciousness becomes more real that what has been termed "real" so that the dream becomes reality and reality becomes the dream.

of building a home or whatever the dream is. The dream eventually becomes reality and the home becomes a concrete object.

So it is with the ascension. As one seeks that which is happening within, one ascends. One reaches the state of consciousness that is a different paradigm. It has lost its fear. It has lost its pain. It has lost its sorrow. It has lost its control. It has lost all the things that are shed like an animal that sheds a skin. It is gone. It goes away and the animal remains. The superficial needs to do anything except follow the path within—fade away, fall off. The "scales before the eyes" is the image used within the Biblical context. So the ascension occurs within. The dream becomes reality.

Then you ask the question, "To what end?" It is the realization of that which exists within. It is the coming full circle. It is the realization of that which was never left, cannot be left, could never be left, that which exists permanently. And that which seemed so permanent is only a paradigm. It is only a temporary state of consciousness.

You will see that the earth is truly shifting. It is changing very, very rapidly and you do not understand that it is changing from within. That is the concept that is impossible to understand. It cannot be emphasized enough that it is not changing from without. It is only changing from within—the mass of the earth, the strength of the earth, the power of the earth all exists within the individual. That is the most difficult of all to understand because within the traditions of religions, they have sought to diminish that power, that strength, that permanence, that understanding that exists within the individual and sought to discount it so that many religions say, "I am only a humble sinner. I am only weak, but thou art strong." But that is not the way it works, simply put. It is quite the opposite. The individual is the strength of the earth. The individual is the power of the earth. The individual is unlimited love. The individual is beyond imagination in terms of the power that exists within. It is presence within the Presence. It cannot be anything short of the greatest power there is so the idea that the individual is weak and unable to make its own decisions and is malleable and must rely on the religions then is a disservice to the nature of the individual, to the power within the child, to the power within moment, to the power within the present time. There is only the power within the Power and the myth is vanishing. There is only the love within Love. There is only the life within Life. There is only the truth within Truth. It is all in the power of what has been termed God. It is all within. It is not without.

The world as you know it is made up of objects, of things, and you have termed that the "physical world" and you have then determined that there is a "metaphysical world" and what is not understood is that is not the case, that physical world emerges from the metaphysical world and they are one. The oneness of all life, the oneness of time, the oneness the Presence within the present, the oneness of all is not a myth. It is a fact.

There is a oneness that supersedes the oneness that you have determined within your own consciousness. It is like the air that you breathe is one with you and yet remains its own air and that is similar to what happens with the oneness of all. It is all part of the whole and yet has distinct differences. The way that you understand the oneness of all is when you meditate or pray or go within then it suddenly does occur to you that there is something else, and yet, you see that within the present time so that you experience the present time and understand oneness and then out in the image on the mirror, you have this concept called oneness, but it is not the same as the oneness within the present time. There is no line of demarcation. There is no defining oneness. It only exists within the individual at that point. All exists within the individual. So the image on the mirror shows that all life is one and is spoken of within this context, but all life is one and it is within the consciousness of the present time that you actually experience that oneness. It cannot be experienced within the image on the mirror. So individuals preach oneness, but they do not understand the nature of the integrated whole within the individual.

Empathy is understanding the nature of oneness. Empathy exists within the heart. Empathy does not exist within the head. One cannot empathize with another's situation within the head. One has to within the heart of the individual. It is so with oneness as well. It is not inward from the sense that there only one being together and we are all in this together, particularly the individual does not necessarily believe that. It is the understanding within the present time, within the moment of the nature of all being, together.

You will see that the life that you have created for yourself is that of the dreamer in the dream. It is the illusion within the truth. It is the life within the life. It is the love within love itself. It is the dream within the dreamer. The dreamer is more than you can imagine. The imagination is more than you can imagine. The truth is much, much more than you can imagine. It is omnipresent. It is with you at all times, in all places, but the illusion becomes very

You will see that the life that you have created for yourself is that of the dreamer in the dream. It is the illusion within the truth. It is the life within the life. It is the love within love itself. It is the dream within the dreamer. The dreamer is more than you can imagine.

important to you, to the point where you feel you must maintain the illusion over the truth itself. It becomes a missionary zeal to maintain the illusion at all cost. Therefore, you fight for whatever theological beliefs you hold, or whatever political beliefs you hold, so that the dream remains, but the truth exists within you and there is a point that is coming very soon in which you will not be able to resist the need for the truth itself and you will allow the illusion to vanish.

You will allow the dream to be released. You will allow the river of life to flow as it must. What happens, in a sense, that you create little dams in the river of love itself in order to feel that you control the dream. The flow itself is the life you experience; it is the energy you experience; It is the love you experience. It is the truth you experience. It has its own energy. It has its own flow. It has its own life. To allow it to happen in its own way would be to give up the illusion of your existence. When you meditate you are at one with your existence. You are at peace with your existence. It exists within its own natural state, but when you allow the dream to take over and control your existence, then all of the illusions that create pain, that create sorrow, that create fear, seem to be in the way of this flow, of this truth of the nature of your own being. Part of what is understood to be the ascension is to release that dream, to not define life, to let life become, as theologians have said, "the will of God," the life of God within the present time, therefore, for example, the story about the lilies of the field, that God provides for them is really the nature of life itself., that the provision is there. There is fear that it is not there, but it is there. It is created to be there. If one looks at a beautiful mountain scene, one understands that it is created to be there. It is a natural state. It is abundant. It is flowing. It is at peace with itself. It is at one with itself. It is within the perimeters of its own being. So it is with life as it goes through the ascension. It is the releasing of so many small dams in the river. It is the releasing of illusions. It is the releasing of the dream to become the natural state of the individual. Nothing is lost. Nothing is contrived. Nothing is shot and then found. It simply is in the state of being that exists within the present time within existence itself and the dream and the dreamer are released to become at one with the whole. It exists all of the time. What you don't understand yet is that existence exists within itself and is undying. It simply exists within itself. Your existence exists within itself. Life's existence exists within itself. And there is nothing else. There is nothing but that being. The illusion is gone. The dream is gone. The dreamer is gone. The existence simply exists within itself within its most natural state.

You will see that the way is becoming so very clear to those who are understanding the nature of the present time, the nature of the truth of being, the nature of their power as individuals. It is like looking into a beautiful well of water and seeing all that exists reflected back into your own eyes which, in fact, reflect back into the water. It is a joyous, beautiful experience for the individual to see life within life, to see the dreamer within the dream and understand the crystalline nature of the entire experience. It is free of all of the encumbrances that have existed before the

You will see that the way is becoming so very clear to those who are understanding the nature of the present time, the nature of the truth of being, the nature of their power as individuals. It is like looking into a beautiful well of water and seeing all that exists reflected back into your own eyes which, in fact, reflect back into the water.

moment of looking into the water and seeing your own life within life, your own love within love, your own truth within truth itself. It is the moment of oneness that you have longed for within your heart because it exists within your heart. It does not exist within the mind. It exists within the moment of understanding, of joy, of experience itself. The life within the dream is life. It is all that ever will exist. It is timeless. It has no time. It has no limits. It has total freedom from the fear, from the lack, from the pain, from the sorrow. It is free of all encumbrances. It is truly the shedding of the skin. It is truly the falling of the veil before the eyes. It is everything that has been described numerous times, but it has actually been experienced globally so that there is nothing that holds it back. There is nothing that keeps it from becoming what it is in its own crystalline form. There is no shadow. There is no fog. There is no sadness. There is no sorrow. It is simply is free of all encumbrances and that all exists and has existed within the present time.

You will see that as the world emerges from the world of fear to the world of love, it is not conscious. The reason that it is unconscious is the same reason that has been described before. When this occurs, it does not occur within the image on the mirror. It occurs before that emerges. In many ways, what you have called the conscious mind is the image on the mirror and it is not the moment of truth. It is not the moment of life. It is not the moment of love. It is the conscious mind—the remembrance of the moment, so that as the occurrence takes place within the present time, within the Presence. It is instantaneous. It is revolutionary.

You will see that the dreamer and the dream cease to separate. They cease to be anything but the oneness that exists. You will see it is like a tree that blossoms. It is like a plant that grows rapidly in the sunshine. It reaches the light. It utilizes the light. It processes the light so very rapidly because it is growing as rapidly as the light will allow. It is joyous. It is hard to understand that as a plant has all of the nutrients and the light it needs, it is in a joyous state. The kind of growth that occurs then for the plant is one of joy. It is with you as well. Imagine that you are alone with yourself. Imagine that you have come to a point of utter joy, of utter peace, of utter oneness with yourself. Imagine that that state exists without limit, that you are one with others who are also in that state of being. It is this transformation that occurs. The images that one experiences are no longer the images on the mirror. The imagery is that of the beauty that exists within. Imagine being lost in the most beautiful painting you ever saw—just the moment you are struck by the painting. Imagine entering a valley with the sun shining upon the water. Imagine a place within yourself that is at peace. Imagine looking at the face of a child.

In many ways, what you have called the conscious mind is the image on the mirror and it is not the moment of truth. It is not the moment of life. It is not the moment of love. It is the conscious mind—the remembrance of the moment, so that as the occurrence takes place within the present time, within the Presence.

Imagine loving someone with complete abandon. All of those things are images that emerge from the state of being that exist within each individual—that exist within all life. It is real. It is not hypothetical. It exists. What is hypothetical is the image on the mirror because it is malleable, because it is changeable, because it becomes a drama that plays itself out. But the reality is what exists within the individual and the dream and the dreamer are one. The emergence of that being, of that state, of that awareness is the ascension. It is literally crowding out the other experiences. They are, in a sense, being pushed away because the old state of being in which you actually existed within the state of being described is diminishing. A good way of staying within the presence of the Presence is to go within a remembrance of joy in your life. In a sense, you actually move physically into that state. You actually remove yourself physically from the other state of being then move into the other state of being yourself. It is actually what you term a physical occurrence. It is when you move into the heart that you actually begin to function more and more within the heart. It is the closet that Jesus referred to when he said, "Go into your closet and shut the door." That is actually the state of being described. That is the state of being that heals. That is the state of being that corrects the image on the mirror. That is the state of being that brings others within the same state of being within themselves. It is the moment of prayer. It is the moment of petition. It is the moment of meditation. It is the moment of acknowledgment within the individual so that the image on the mirror is affected in a positive way. It is transformed because the only place that existence occurs is within thought so that the thought occurs, the transformation occurs, the changes occur within. They exist within the presence, within the love within the love and that love becomes magnified within exponentially so that the individual is expanded to their actual nature within.

The most difficult concept for you to understand is that the earth exists within the individual and not that the individual exists within the earth. It is much like the revelation of Copernicus that contradicted those who believed that the sun revolved around the earth, but, in fact, that is not the case.

You will see that the "New Earth" is simply the earth within. It is the life within. It is the spirit within. It has never left the individual. It exists as a concept long before it exists as a prophesy or a message. It is unchanging. That which is considered prophesy is that which is unchanging. That which is considered a revelation is that which is unchanging and has always existed within the individual. It is not "New Earth," it is within the being of the individual. The most difficult concept for you to understand is that the earth exists within the individual Not that the individual exists within the earth. It is much like the revelation of Copernicus that contradicted those who believed that the sun revolved around the earth, but, in fact, that is not the case. It is the case here for the individual to understand that all beauty, all life, all truth, of what you experience is within and the way to discover further what is to be discovered is to go within, not without. It is the place of all scientific discoveries. It is the place of all metaphysical revelation. It is the place of all humanitarian effort. It is the place of all human kindness. It is the place of all description and exploration of existence. If that singular point is truly understood, that is the point of ascension. But the understanding is not the intellectual understanding. It is

The most difficult concept for you to understand is that the earth exists within the individual and not that the individual exists within the earth. It is much like the revelation of Copernicus that contradicted those who believed that the sun revolved around the earth, but, in fact, that is not the case.

within the being of the individual. It is the dreamer within the dream. It is the presence within the Presence.

The world does not see the vision of what is coming. It cannot visualize the nature of the ascension. It is beyond any image that has been created within any image that has been created within the human consciousness. It is like a child trying to describe to the mother what the imagination the child has. The language is lacking to describe the nature of what the child was imagining and the mother has not yet taught the language to the child to convey that information and when the child grows to the point where that information can be conveyed, then the child no longer carries the image in the same way. It is not difficult to understand why the image is beyond the imagination at this point because the world is so encumbered within its own collective awareness that it cannot see the nature of its own being truly. It cannot see the depth of the love, compassion, kindness, purity, spirit, mind, intellect, all the things that are encompassed within the larger being. It has forgotten the child within. It has forgotten the unlimited nature of its own being, but it remembers it within the present. It exists within the present, so that, at the moment, before the individual is hit by the wave, for example, that moment exists so it is not important in the image on the mirror, that the visualization occurs. It is only important that individuals meditate. It is only important that they go away and return to this plane of existence.

You will see that the world does not see the vision of what is coming. It cannot visualize the nature of the ascension. It is beyond any image that has been created within any image that has been created within the human consciousness.

It is all that matters at this point. The preparation is there.

There are those who assume that if you act correctly, that, for example, if you are kind to one another that ascension will occur. They do not understand the nature of the present time. They do not understand the nature of unlimited thinking. They do not understand the nature of the larger being and so assume that this life is a direct reflection of the larger being, that is not so. This life is a direct reflection of all of the beliefs that have been accumulated by the individual. It is nothing more, but it is not the nature of the present time. It is not the nature of the ascension, nor is it the nature of the larger being. There is hope in that. There is understanding in that. There is truth in that so the preparation that occurs is that of meditation, is that of prayer, is that of enjoyment, is that of peace within. That is all that is required. It is not proving to the image on the mirror that there is a larger being. It is not necessary. It exists—like life exists, like sunlight exists, like flowers exists, like moonlight exists, like everything you accept exists—the larger being exists and is existent within the nature of the present time.

12

The Way, the Truth, and the Life

You will see that when Jesus referred to the term, "I am the way, the truth, and the life," it is like referring to a great, great, difficult to even imagine, room, space present in time, white hole, as opposed to black hole, dimension. It is referred to in this book as the nature of the present time. It is placed in the present time by the use of the words, "I am." It is not as theologians have discussed. It is not a secular thought. It is within the heart. It is within the larger being. It is the nature of the larger being itself that exists—that does not project itself upon the mirror, that is incapable of being limited to the image upon the mirror and so what happens within this experience is that the image picks up a being of that present nature, a moment, a moment before you are hit by the wave, that exists, and so, for sometimes within a flash of a second within this experience on this plane of existence, individuals have that moment and they call it "revelation" and they call it the presence of the Presence within their experience within the image on the mirror.

That leads the way to theological beliefs, and, ironically, the belief system limits the individual to the image on the mirror because the image on the mirror is composed of those theological beliefs that the individual has, so that "the way, the truth, and the life" is incapable of being within this experience, and, yet, it is almost that, "beyond this experience, within this experience," can exist and is emerging within the consciousness, within the thought, within the reality of the individual at this time. It is occurring rapidly. It is universal. It is not limited to human life. It is unlimited in all ways. It is like light that goes out in all directions into space and light years away can be perceived so that it is not limited to this place and time and mentality, or what is perceived of as mentality. That beam of light, that presence within the Presence, that revelation, that way, is all there is. There is nothing else. It is the reality of existence. It has never entered within the image on the mirror as it is now. It is the "second coming" within each individual. The truth of the life within, the life of the life within—all those simply exist. They always have, always will, so exist within the present

You will see that when Jesus referred to the term, "I am the way, the truth, and the life," it is like referring to a great, great, difficult to even imagine, room, space present in time, white hole, as opposed to black hole, dimension. It is referred to in this book as the nature of the present time. It is placed in the present time by the use of the words, "I am." It is not as theologians have discussed. It is not a secular thought. It is within the heart. It is within the larger being.

time. The symbology begins to disappear. The images, in their own way, begin to waiver, begin to transform themselves so that experiences become different for individuals. The wish that they always dreamed of, comes true. The presence within their heart becomes enlarged within their own being, within their own experience here.

You will simply allow it to happen. You will flow with it. You will dance with it. You will play, enjoy. You will not be afraid of it. You will meditate more frequently. That is the only change you will see within the next short period of time.

You will see that way that is described in the Bible is not the traditions of the churches. It is not the way of the image on the mirror. It is the way of the universe of love. It exists within love itself. It is like a pathway. It is a like a walkway to remove oneself from the image and rejoin the individuals within the present time—within the presence within the Presence. It has been translated into the person of Jesus or Mohammed or Buddha, but it is not within that person. It is within the way, itself. It is within the Presence, itself. It is the moment that the individual understands everything. It is i the moment that the individual sees everything, feels everything, and it occurs frequently. The individual is not removed from it. It is not taken from them by circumstances. It is exists within. It is the heart. It is the love. It is the permanence that exists within the individual. It is, in fact, the nature of the individual. So when the Bible says, "I am the way, the truth, and the life," it is within each individual. It is not exterior to that individual. It is the truth. And whatever mythology, and whatever belief system, and whatever context

You will see that way that is described in the Bible is not the traditions of the churches.

and whatever sadness exists within the image on the mirror, it does not exist within the individual because the individual is permanently within that state of love. It is the way, the truth, and the life because that is the only place life exists. It does not exist within the image on the mirror. It is very difficult to understand, but when one is taking away life or adding life or whatever, that is only an image on the mirror. It is only an image of the life. It is not the nature of the life so that when one encounters "the way, the truth, and the life," one encounters it within.

The ascension occurs when that permanent part of the individual, when "the way, the truth, and the life" only exists, and there is nothing else. That is the ascension. That is the "rapture." That is all the things that the churches have talked about, but it is not within this plane of existence. It is within the individual. It is occurring rapidly, within, not exterior, but within. You will see that there is nothing but the presence of the Presence—it is the Son of God—it is the manifestation of God that exists within. It is the "second coming" within. It is the life within. It is the soul within. It is the love within.

It is important to take part of the day and feel that love within. Take the moment to feel the existence of the heart. Take the moment to feel the presence of the love within the heart and understand that that is all there is.

You will see that the entire process of which was spoken is accelerating at this point. You are accelerating at this point. You are growing rapidly like the plant that is in the sunlight that has been in a dark room. You are growing very, very rapidly and it is difficult for you to imagine how quickly this is occurring for you. It is not within a linear time sequence. It is within, within—within your being. It is like the plant that has blossomed. The blossom has emerged and the beauty of the plant is apparent for all to see. It is like the society in which you live is becoming a beautiful field of wild flowers. It is that the blossoming is occurring around you in place around you even in places where you felt that it could not. It is occurring rapidly for others as well. You remain catalysts for this enormous change, but the change is occurring within each individual. It is their ascension. It is their blossoming as well. You will see that there is much to be done rapidly in order for the mist to rise, for the fog to lift. The way, the truth and the life is omnipresent. It is within. It exists.

You will see that the way is complete for humanity and all life. It is like a circle that has come full circle. It is a complete thing that has its own cycle, its own place. The books will help humanity in this period. They will expand greatly across the planet, not because of the individuals involved, but because of the nature of reality, the nature of being. The cycle that is being completed within the individual beings upon this plane of existence is difficult to imagine because there is not the vocabulary for the experience—because the experience has not been completed. It is only after the experience is completed that the vocabulary develops to explain the experience. And, therefore, the words that describe the experience of the image on the mirror are easy to understand because the cycle was completed for those who were experiencing the events, but when

You will see that churches have evolved as a rationale and the language of liturgy and traditions have evolved within, to some degree, the image on the mirror. They remain as a history, as an experience of those who lived within the present. It is the great masters who lived within the present, who did not live within the image.

the event has not been completed, the vocabulary has not been developed so it is only an image (using imagery such as simile or metaphor) can describe what is happening. And thus it (the experience) is more difficult to understand, but it can be seen with, what is termed "the third eye" in the greater being. It can be seen within the present time, within the presence within the Presence.

The way is so very easy at this point within the individual beings. They do understand the ease with which it is all occurring now. It is as if the struggle were over. It is as if they were swimming gently to the shore, having come down a rapids. It is as if there were peace, actually possible, for the individual, after having been through a war, in effect, but the way is becoming easier for individuals, collectively, as well. And it is as if those things which are violent, which are painful, which are frightening, which are suffering are slowly being shuffed off, deliberately, and as the fog rises, the pain diminishes until there is no more pain, actually, within this plane of existence. It is becoming what has been envisioned as "the golden age," but it is within consciousness. It is within thought. It is within each individual. It is not within the collective awareness, nor the collective memory that these things occur. It is like when a child is playing. It is not that the child deliberately becomes joyous. They simply play and joy is a part of the play.

So it is with the experiences now. It is not that the individuals become deliberately peaceful, or their lives become easier, it is simply within the individual that these things occur and the ebullience and the effervescence and the joy that occur, occur naturally and are not contrived or deliberate. They simply well up out of the individual because the individual is becoming closer and closer to their own being, to the presence within the Presence, to the present time and existing less and less within the image on the mirror so that the ambitions of the image on the mirror or the pain of the image on the mirror, or the power seeking of the image on the mirror, or the divisions, or the delusions, or the myths, or the history, even, of the image on the mirror becomes less and less important. And, the present becomes more and more a reality. As one becomes engrossed in the present, one becomes more and more in tune with their own being—within their joy, within the nature of their unlimited love and begin to discover the massiveness of their own being, of their own kindness, of their own love, of their own truths and it is, truly, truly, a joyous process for individuals and they reach a point where they cannot be dragged back into the image on the mirror because they no longer seek it within themselves. It is freedom for each individual.

You will see that churches have evolved as a rationale and the language of liturgy and traditions have evolved within, to some degree, the image on the mirror. They remain as a history, as an experience of those who lived within the present. It is the great masters who lived within the present, who did not live within the image. They lived within the life, within the being, within the presence of the Divine within themselves and as they lived within that moment, within that millisecond before awareness, the world could recognize the teachings they had to offer, then they took those teachings and created traditions. There is nothing wrong with traditions, but it is just not the same as the inspiration that created the traditions to start with. And, it is only within the present time within the presence of the Presence of God within that the individual feels the love that actually is taught within the churches. It is like a child who loves their parents with all of their heart, or an animal, or a flower. It is an action of the heart , itself, it is not and action of the mind or a deliberate thing in any way, shape, or form. It is the presence within the child that experiences that joy. So it is within you, as individuals, at this point. It is like the child has emerged within your own being and the joy of that child. It is really quite simple and contained within the heart. It is not an intellectual thing. It is of the heart. It is within the heart. It is something when one talks about the heart. It is one when one actually feels the experience.

So, the present time is where the ascension occurs. It does not occur anywhere else. It does not occur within theological teachings. It does not occur within a religion. It does not occur within a given group. It only occurs, very childlike, within the heart of the being within the present time and it always occurs. It is always occurring. It is not a moment in time in which it occurs. It is ongoing within the individual, within the heart, within the present time.

But, freedom within the individual means that the individual is truly within the present time. It is within its own being. It is within its higher self. It sees the world through the heart.

The world has completed its own cycle, in a sense, which is hard, again, for you to envision because as the cycle is completed, the world begins to absorb the significance of the cycle within the image on the mirror. It is beginning to understand the nature of the ascension. It is beginning to understand the nature of what freedom actually means within the individual, not freedom within a political sense. It is different. But, freedom within the individual means that the individual is truly within the present time. It is within its own being. It is within its higher self. It sees the world through the heart. Its understands the world as being "heart-felt," as being loved, as being animated by its own emotions and shapes? and so the image is free of encumbrances and of painful experiences and anything that would keep it from operating in the present time. It is unconscious thought. It is not conscious thought. It is not rational. It is not described well. It is described poorly, at the very best, because it occurs within meditation. It occurs within prayer. It occurs within the individual being, not exterior to the heart of the individual. It is like a large, white silk blanket that is thrown over everything so the individual experiences nothing but the peace of the experience itself divorced from imagery, divorces from ego, divorced from pain, divorce from anything but the light of love from within. It is free. The freedom that occurs is not the political freedom where there is a constitution. It is simply within the individual as a freedom of love. The freedom that occurs when one loves completely.

The world is ready for this work. It is anxious to see this work. It is a shift within consciousness that is difficult to articulate, but it is, nonetheless, true. It is, nonetheless always there. It does not detract from it that humanity has sought many religions and many ways to find what exists within. It does not detract from the reality of existence. It only means that as humanity walks many, many paths it still was in existence and walking the paths were almost of no consequence. What mattered was the life, the love, the truth, the soul, the spirit within the individual. And THAT was the reality. That was the consciousness. That was the divine. That was all that truly was. The path was almost irrelevant. It only was the way that was walked by being of light, the being of truth,

You will see that the world is ready for this work. It is anxious to see this work. It is a shift within consciousness that is difficult to articulate, but it is, nonetheless, true.

the being of soul. That is what mattered after all. The world is beginning to understand that the individual is what mattered. The path was not. The history was not as important as the presence of life, the presence of love, the presence of truth within the individual consciousness. That was, ultimately, what it was all about.

As humanity ascends it simply continues to exist within that light, that love, that truth, that soul, and the fog surrounding it lifts. The path is no longer needed through the fog. It is clear for the individual to see as far as they need to see. It is clear for them to become all that they are. It is not necessary for them to seek guidance from without. It is only necessary to meditate and pray and seek guidance from within each individual on this plane of existence. The meditation, the prayer, the love, the kindness, the moment before you are hit by a wave, is all that is effecting this plane of existence at this time. It is very important that that prayer continue, that that meditation, that being that exists continue at this time. It is of extreme importance that individuals continue the path that they have chosen and as the fog lifts, they will see that it was never the religion. It was never the doctrine. It was never the tradition. It was never the teaching. It was always love... within the heart, that mattered.

You will see that those who have seen the light have returned, but not returned. They remain at one with the experience that they have had.

There is much to do yet, but it is simpler. It is easier. It less complicated than it has been before.

Those who have seen the light have returned, but not returned. They remain at one with the experience that they have had. That is true of many who have had died and returned or had an awakening and returned. They simply remained in the state in which they were in when they left this experience. They truly went home. They ascended. They reached that place within themselves that they have always sought within themselves, so that it is not important to them that the world become corrected in every little way. The understanding that the world is the temporary place and what exists within is the permanence of the individual. It is a difficult concept to understand because it exists every day, all the time. It does not cease to exist within the individual as they live their lives. It remains within them. It is a clarity. It is an understanding. It is a purity. It is a kindness. It is a wisdom. It is many things, but it exists within, not without the individual and they truly do understand that is the case. As the ascension occurs, it occurs within. It occurs on a constant basis within. It does occur at some point in time in which humanity is lifted up. It occurs all of the time. It is within. It is just that when what is called the ascension then that part of the individual within is entered into and it remains within the individual. It is not affected by others. It is not affected by time. It is affected by circumstances. It is not affected by religious dogma. It is not affected by anything, but what exists within the individual and it is truly omnipresent. It is all knowing, all seeing, all kind, all true, without pain, without sorrow.